RIVERS

ESTABLISHING *the* APOSTOLIC MINDSET

FROM EDEN

MARTIJN VAN TILBORGH

KUDU

Rivers from Eden: Establishing the Apostolic Mindset
by Martijn van Tilborgh

Copyright © 2006 by Martijn van Tilborgh

Cover design by Martijn van Tilborgh
Published by Kudu Publishing

Print ISBN: 9781938624599
eBook ISBN: 9781938624605

Rivers from Eden is also available on Amazon Kindle, Barnes
& Noble Nook and Apple iBooks.

CONTENTS

ACKNOWLEDGMENTS

Thank you to our spiritual family all over the world, for your support and friendship. There are too many names to mention. Thanks also to family and friends throughout the world who, through the years, have supported us faithfully even, when we were making decisions that were at times unconventional. And thanks to my wife, Amy, for your love, support, and readiness to follow the leading of the Spirit at all times!

INTRODUCTION

When you think of the Garden of Eden, what picture comes to mind? Many envision an utopian paradise where all of mankind's needs were met at all times. Perhaps a place where Adam and Eve could relax all day and enjoy the warm, sunny weather. Perhaps they led a passive life, without the boredom that we encounter when life is the same day after day. Maybe they didn't even know what was to be bored, because they lived in a perfect world. This understanding of the first days of mankind could best be described as like an extended vacation to a tropical island in the Indian Ocean. Many times the church looks back at this period of time and wishes we were still in such a place. "If only Eve hadn't eaten from that tree!" people may think. Although some of the elements described in the picture above may be accurate, most Christians have a distorted view of the early days of mankind.

Today's utopian view of Eden suggests that we are now subject to sin, hatred, sickness, and disaster because we are living in contrast to that perfect world. Although most of us are confronted with these problems on a daily basis, we need to realize that there is actually not that big a difference between the authority and mandate God gave Adam and the authority and mandate He has given us. We're living in very exiting times as God's Spirit is propelling His church further and further into one of the last phases of the fulfillment of His plan for creation.

When we become aware of this reality, we will align ourselves with what God is doing in this hour and yield ourselves to the destiny He has for our lives.

This book is about the apostolic mandate that God has given to His church, and shows us how we can fulfill this mandate through apostolic reformation. This requires anything but a passive attitude. The word "apostle" (or *apostolos*) means "a delegate," "messenger," "one sent forth with orders." In the following chapters we'll discover that the origin of the apostolic mandate is found in the first chapter of Genesis and that this mandate still rests upon the shoulders of the saints today. It gives us the authority to establish His Kingdom in the earth, and to fill the nations with His glory. Throughout the entire Bible we read about God's desire to send His people out to the four corners of the world, to declare His government and to demonstrate His kingdom.

This desire to take dominion and be fruitful was first revealed through the natural location where God placed Adam and Eve on the sixth day of creation. It sent a clear message of God's destiny for mankind. Genesis 2 tells us that a river went out of Eden and that from there it parted and became four riverheads.

This is a powerful picture of the apostolic mandate revealed in the first book of the Bible—the river flowing from Eden caused the water to go towards the four corners of the earth! The water wasn't contained within the borders of Eden, but it flowed into the whole world. The Garden of Eden was only the beginning. The garden was small in comparison to the face of the earth. It was a place of divine government, glory and perfection. It was the primal example of God's intentions for the rest of the earth. God's presence and government was in the garden, but it couldn't just stay there. It had to go out! So God commissioned mankind to take whatever was in that garden and establish that same environment in the four corners of the world.

This apostolic mandate and anointing was purposed to lead to the fulfillment of the ultimate plan and purpose of God for creation: to establish divine government in the nations. We live in a time in which God is restoring the office of the apostle to His church. He is raising up apostles from around the world who will release a new move of His Spirit. A thorough reformation is taking place in the church as these men and women of God begin declaring His plan for this time.

The intention of this book is to journey through the different aspects of this current apostolic reformation, and to show how it is influencing the church. We will read about how this reformation is changing our old wineskins into new wineskins that will be able to contain the new wine of this apostolic movement. My prayer is that, through this book, our old mindsets will continue to be transformed and aligned with the current revelation that God's Spirit is releasing in this day. This transformation will cause a river of God's Spirit to come forth from His church that will send countless men and women of God to the different regions of the world. With the apostolic mandate on their shoulders, these people of God will execute His purposes in the earth, elevating our societies to the standard of God and reaching the uttermost parts of the earth.

THE RIVER AND THE HIGH PLACE

The "river" is a clear metaphor used throughout the whole Bible to illustrate the move of God's Spirit. In Genesis 2:10-14 we read that in the Garden of Eden a river parted into four riverheads:

Now a river went out of Eden to water the garden, and from there it parted and became four riverheads. The name of the first is Pishon; it is the one which skirts the whole land of Havilah, where there is gold. And the gold of that land is good. Bdellium and the onyx stone are there. The name of the second river is Gihon; it is the one which goes around the whole land of Cush. The name of the third river is Hiddekel; it is the one which goes toward the east of Assyria. The fourth river is the Euphrates.

A river always flows from a high place to a lower place. Eden must have been located on a high place in order for the river to flow from it. "The high place" in the Bible is identified as a location of intimacy between God and men. Moses had a glorious encounter with God after he reached the high place on Mount Sinai (Exod. 24:18). The same was true for Elijah when God revealed Himself in a still, small voice on top of Mount Horeb (1 Kings 19:12-13). Altars were built and sacrifices were made on high places. We find this picture of interaction between men and God at high places throughout the Bible.

In the same way, as God inhabits the praises of His people, we can identify the high place under the new covenant as the church of Christ. A river will come forth, from wherever God is enthroned. Wherever His throne is established, a stream of life will flow out from that place. For example, God's throne was established in Eden. We also read in Ezekiel that a river came forth from the temple, the place from which God governed His people (Ezek. 47:1-5). In the New Testament a river of living water springs forth from our innermost being (John 4:14). This is because we have now become His temple; the Holy Spirit inhabits our being. In Revelation 22:1 we read that a river flows from the throne of God. The ultimate desire of God is for a river to come forth from the place where His throne is established. And this river must then flow to the four corners of the earth.

Chapter 1

GOD'S ETERNAL ASSIGNMENT

. . . .

The apostolic anointing enables us to fulfill God's plan and purposes in the earth. To have an accurate understanding of why God is restoring the apostolic anointing in our generation, and why this radical reformation is necessary, we need to lay a good foundation concerning "dominion theology." Once this foundation is properly laid we will be more able to place apostolic reformation in its historical time perspective. We will begin to more accurately understand where we are on the prophetic timetable of the Lord. So let's start at the beginning.

THE APOSTOLIC MANDATE

I noted in the introduction that the picture of a passive Adam and Eve in the Garden of Eden is inaccurate. A distorted understanding of their situation influences our entire view of God's eternal plan and purpose for mankind. Adam received a clear, threefold assignment from God, and with this mandate he was sent into the world. In other words, there was work to do! This might sound a little strange. Why would God situate man in a place where they would still need to work? Wouldn't mean that His creation was not that "perfect" after all? The reason for this decision was that, in His desire to have fellowship with men, God wanted Adam to participate in what He was doing. God gave Adam the assignment and authority to finish what He had started, and also to bring those things to perfection.

We find the first assignment in Genesis 1:28:

Then God blessed them, and God said to them, "Be fruitful and multiply; fill the earth."

This instruction is clear: they had to multiply by giving birth to sons and daughters. God didn't want Adam and Eve to sit around under an Eden palm tree. He wanted them to become a people that would multiply and fill the entire earth.

The second assignment can be found in the second part of that same verse:

... fill the earth and subdue it; have dominion over the fish of the sea, over the birds of the air, and over every living thing that moves on the earth."

God didn't just tell Adam and Eve to govern over the garden alone. No, the mandate was to subdue the entire earth. To rule over Eden wasn't really a problem for them. The garden was already a place where divine government had been established. If that was all they had needed to do, they would've simply maintained that which was already there. But no, they needed to go and extend God's government from the garden and take it to the four corners of the world. They had to go and take dominion over the rest of the earth. Eden was the model they were supposed to use as a standard in subduing the world.

The third and last assignment God gave is seen in Genesis 2:19:

Out of the ground the Lord God formed every beast of the field and every bird of the air, and brought them to Adam to see what he would call them. And whatever Adam called each living creature, that was its name.

A person's name speaks of their identity. So we see how God had Adam participate in the finishing touch of His creation. He gave him responsibility to prophesy identity to part of creation. Not just to the animals in the garden, but to every created beast on the earth.

Adam was the first person sent by God to work out this threefold mandate. He was clearly "sent forth with orders," received from God personally. Therefore we could say that Adam was the first apostle in history.

We can see that when God created mankind, He had a clear plan and a clear purpose in mind. This hasn't changed:

- He still wants His people, the church, to reproduce so that they multiply and fill the earth.

- He still wants His people to rule and reign on the earth, having dominion over every demonic influence, and establishing divine government in the nations.

- He still wants His people to be a prophetic people that will speak identity and destiny in the world around them.

THE AUTHORITY TO RULE AND REIGN

The words "mandate" and "authority" are two words that cannot be separated. Without authority it is impossible to fulfill a mandate. That is why God gave Adam and Eve a position of absolute authority, which then enabled them to work out every detail of their assignment. Not only were they given the crown of creation, they were also given the position of wearing it as rulers over creation. They were made kings, created to govern the earth.

However, when you fail to step into your God-given authority, someone else will take it and use it against you. The reality of this principle is revealed throughout the Bible. In disobedience, Adam and Eve left their position of authority. The result was that Satan took possession of their void in the realm of the spirit, exercising his authority in the position that had originally been given to mankind. Instead of a divine government that was supposed to be established through men, Satan started ruling over the earth and mankind. The result of his destructive reign was the manifestations of sin, sickness, division, and death. Satan had taken dominion. Now that darkness had captured the scepter to rule over the earth, men could no longer stay in the garden. Mankind had to be removed from the presence of God. They were unable to have the same fellowship as before, and were banned from that river of life that would take them to the nations.

GOD'S UNCHANGING PURPOSES

Despite the stagnation that was caused by the fall of man, God was determined to use him to fulfill the mandate He had given. Even after Adam messed up, God didn't change His mind. This is very important to understand. The very moment God declares something, He will guard that word and fulfill it. It will not return void, but will manifest sooner or later. When God uttered His apostolic purpose for mankind to live a life of multiplication and dominion, He released an unstoppable thrusting power in the realm of the spirit that moves towards the fulfillment of those words. They are full of the energy of God Himself, and are moving and living in the heavenlies. Even through the centuries they will remain alive, waiting patiently for a doorway to open through which they can manifest themselves in the natural realm. But when we lack this understanding of the power of God's Word, it will be impossible for us to fully see why God did the things He did throughout history.

God's purpose is still to have the three assignments He gave to Adam and Eve completed. The words from the first chapter of Genesis are still very much alive and will not return void. Throughout the ages they have influenced and touched different generations.

These words have stirred up and touched the hearts of men for better and for worse. Because God spoke these words into mankind, the desire to rule and reign has remained deeply rooted in the hearts of men. Depending on who is in authority over our lives, we can either establish God's kingdom and His glory in the earth, or by plugging in to the domain of darkness, we can manifest demonic government.

Once we understand this we need to lay down every passive attitude that keeps us from fulfilling our destiny. God's kingdom won't just drop from the sky and suddenly make the world a better place. No, in order to see God's plan unfold in our lifetime we need to actively pick up the mandate that God has purposed for us to carry and begin to see our generation being transformed by the power of the Holy Spirit. The destiny He has for us surpasses anything we can think or pray. Many Scriptures confirm this process. In Acts 3:21 we read:

> *Whom heaven must receive until the times of restoration of all things, which God has spoken by the mouth of all His holy prophets since the world began.*

There are two things that we can conclude from this portion of scripture. First, Jesus is not coming back until "all things" have been restored. What are these "all things?" To have this question answered we need to go back to the beginning of "all things." Before the fall of mankind, there was no need for restoration, simply because creation was perfect. The apostolic mandate that God gave Adam needs to be recovered, restored and fulfilled by the church before Jesus can ever return.

The second thing we can conclude from this passage is that it is not just an isolated remark by the apostle Peter, but that the holy prophets since the beginning of the world have spoken of this principle. This truth is not just valid under the new covenant, but throughout the entire Bible. Everything God has done in history, and all that He will do in the future, can be placed within the unfolding of His eternal plan.

Throughout time, the plan of God unfolds. It reveals itself progressively through the centuries. Every initiative God took in the Old and New Testament builds towards the restoration of all things. Every act of God in the future will build towards that same goal. God's kingdom is one of progression and increase. Isaiah 9:7 teaches:

Of the increase of His government and peace there will be no end.

So there is a constant increase of His kingdom. It will go from glory to glory, from strength to strength. There will be a constant movement and change until God has accomplished His purposes. Every revelation, of course, needs to be in line with the word of God and not just an interesting thought. Every movement of the Holy Spirit causes the will of God to be revealed more accurately.

In Acts 18, we see a clear example of this principle. The apostles met a disciple who knew about the doctrine of baptism in water, but he was not familiar with the baptism of the Holy Spirit. Therefore his understanding of God was limited, and he needed a new revelation in order to be aligned with what God was doing in his time. He knew the teaching of John the Baptist, but he didn't yet have the experience of the baptism in the Holy Spirit. Acts 18:26 gives the following account of this situation:

So he began to speak boldly in the synagogue. When Aquila and Priscilla heard him, they took him aside and explained to him the way of God more accurately.

In the same way, throughout history God has given new revelation and progressive restoration movements that have enabled us to understand His ways more accurately. When we have this more accurate understanding of God's plan, we will be more and more able to execute His purposes in the earth.

DISPENSATIONS AND ESCAPISM

God does not change His plan. He doesn't chop history up, creating different theological dispensations. So often we categorize events into independent, isolated periods of time, as if God changed His mind for everyone living under these different dispensations. For example, a few dispensations that have been created are the age before the fall, the time after the fall, the time under the law, the time of John the Baptist, the age of the early church, and the millennium of peace. Each of these dispensations is seen as a different, separate, set period of time in which God had decided certain things.

This theology is very fatalistic. It basically concludes that, once you are born under a certain dispensation, you are "doomed" to it. All you can do to see God move is to sit and wait until He declares a new day. For example, people say, "Signs and wonders were for the early church in the book of Acts, but because we are now under a different dispensation we do not have access anymore to the supernatural power of the Holy Spirit." The result of such teaching is that people take on a passive and defensive attitude towards life and the ways of the Spirit. This teaching has caused many Christians to spiritually retreat from the frontlines, and sit and wait for the rapture. They say, "When that happens everything will be better, but until then there is not much we can do!" Instead of seeing the second coming of Christ as the result of a victorious church that walks in dominion, they just hope to escape from this wicked world sometime during their lifetime. This dispensational thinking is called "escapism."

People who place themselves under escapism teaching often isolate themselves and their generation from the eternal plan of God. They place themselves in a position where they are unable to participate in the advancement of that plan. For them, history is not relevant because that was a different dispensation. They cannot influence the future because God has determined the future anyway. In their mind only He decides when it is time for a new dispensation.

It's true that the Bible uses the term "dispensation" several times, in the New Testament. But we have to understand that a true biblical dispensation is not an isolated period of time. More than anything, it is a new era that is ushered in by the progressive nature of God. It is not static, but a dynamic process that develops with the people of God who work with His plan throughout time.

ONE PLAN, DIFFERENT SEASONS

God doesn't change His mind. As a professional master builder, He builds line upon line, precept upon precept. His kingdom becomes more and more visible in the earth. Everything He does today builds upon the foundations of what He did yesterday. Each line will form a foundation for what He will do tomorrow. It is like building a house.

First you lay the foundation and later you place the walls. The walls don't even look like the foundation, yet they are part of the same plan. Only when the walls are up can the roof be placed. At different times, different aspects of the same plan are being built. Both the Old and New Testament consist of different periods of time that are being used as building stones to accomplish the one and only plan of God.

When we fully understand this, we will realize that whatever we actively build for God's kingdom during our lifetime is what we will leave as an inheritance. However, when we stay passive and do nothing, we will add nothing to whatever we have received from our spiritual ancestors. Everything we leave behind in that case is what was already there. An attitude like that will cause stagnation in the advancement of the kingdom of God. It simply means that whatever works God had destined for our generation will shift to the generation after us. This process will continue until a generation is willing to pay the price and pick up the mandate to advance the kingdom of God in the earth. However, an accurate understanding of these dynamics will cause us to give our lives completely for the advancement of God's government in our generation, so that our children will have a rich inheritance with which to work.

The result will be that our children will be greater, more anointed, and more powerful, and they will walk in greater revelation than we ever do. The torch of God's kingdom will be effectively passed from one generation to the next. From Adam to the second coming of Christ it will never go out, but its fire keeps burning bright. Everyone who receives that torch and runs with it becomes part of the frontlines of the army of God that will cause the borders of His kingdom to expand and His glory to increase.

DETERMINE YOUR POSITION

In 1 Chronicles 12:32 we read

Of the sons of Issachar who had understanding of the times, to know what Israel ought to do, their chiefs were two hundred; and all their brethren were at their command.

This verse describes a group of people that were part of the army that was being formed around David when he was fleeing from Saul. The sons of Issachar were those who had the ability to recognize and declare the season that Israel was in. With this valuable prophetic knowledge came understanding, enabling Israel to know which step to take next.

This same gift is given to us in our day. As the plan of God unfolds throughout history, it is important to locate our generation within that plan. What is the season we are in? What is God doing today? It is like locating yourself on a road map. Let's define God's plan as a trip from A to B. It is crucial to know where you are between A and B in order to determine the route ahead of you. Where are we on the road map of God's plan?

Part of knowing God's season comes through the prophetic revelation of the Holy Spirit. The Bible teaches us that God does nothing unless He first reveals it to His servants, the prophets (Amos 3:7). One of the tasks of the office of the prophet is to accurately declare the season of God that is upon us. Another way to recognize the season we are in is by studying history. By knowing the foundation stones that were already laid by our spiritual fathers, we can determine what the next step is going to be.

For example, because we know that in 1906 God restored the baptism of the Holy Spirit back to the Church through the Azusa Street revival, we know that we do not have to fight that battle again because that foundation stone has already been laid by another generation. Because someone else paid the price to see the kingdom advance in that way, we have full access to that experience and truth today.

HONOR YOUR FATHER AND YOUR MOTHER

Most people know the commandment from Exodus 20:12 about honoring your parents: "Honor your father and your mother, that your days may be long upon the land which the Lord your God is giving you." This commandment given through Moses is mainly applied by theologians to our relationship with our natural father and mother.

God promises a long life for those who honor this commandment. But besides the natural interpretation, there is also a spiritual interpretation. When we honor our spiritual forefathers, the patriarchs who went before us, we will stay spiritually alive and will see the promises of God fulfilled for our generation.

God has a destiny for everyone in this world. Every generation is destined to bring creation one step closer to the restoration of all things. Every generation has "a land" that God has promised. To successfully walk in our destiny and calling, we need to honor those ancestors who paid the price in the past, because without them we wouldn't be were we are today.

WHERE ARE WE IN HISTORY?

It is beyond the scope of this book to trace all the moves of the Spirit throughout history. But once we understand the concept of the development of God's plan in the earth, it will be very simple for us to locate the activity of the Spirit throughout the ages on the road map of God.

In Hebrews 11 you can read a general overview of this, most probably written by the apostle Paul. He mentions a list of important "patriarchs of faith" and defines what they have done for the advancement of the kingdom of God. He honors people like Enoch, Abraham, Isaac, Jacob, Joseph, Moses and Gideon. While naming these people, he goes through history until he ends up with himself and his generation. Then he makes the following remark in Hebrews 11:39-40:

And all these, having obtained a good testimony through faith, did not receive the promise, God having provided something better for us, that they should not be made perfect apart from us.

Paul is placing himself and his generation in the lineage of spiritual ancestors, the patriarchs of history. But in doing that he mentions that even though they "obtained a good testimony through faith, that they did not receive the promise." Even though they participated in the plan of God, they never saw the promise of the full restoration.

However, Paul received the spiritual legacy that they left behind, which in turn served as a foundation for his generation and the generations after him to build on, so that plans of God would continue to be accomplished on earth.

Though Adam gave away his authority to Satan, throughout the whole Old Testament God was preparing His people for the recapturing of that stolen position. Through one man (Adam) sin entered the world and through one man (Jesus) atonement from sin was given (Rom. 5:12-17). The Old Testament was a time of preparation, promise, the law, and the prophets. Jesus was the fulfillment of the law and the prophets. He defeated death and Hades, and enabled us to take back the position of authority stolen from us. With that He gave us the ability to once more work out the mandate that was originally placed upon Adam's shoulders.

When we put our faith in Jesus Christ, and when we are born again in Him, we can see the kingdom of God. By believing in the second Adam we are being placed back into the "Garden of Eden," and a place of government and glory becomes our portion. The true church of Jesus Christ is that place. It is the place where people find access to the tree of life, and where God is enthroned on the praises of His people. The church that was founded on the day of Pentecost didn't stop emerging in the earth. Remember, there is a river that flows from that place! This river parts into four river-heads, flowing to the ends of the earth. Jesus confirmed this apostolic mandate by giving the church the following assignment in Mark 16:15-18:

Go into all the world and preach the gospel to every creature. He who believes and is baptized will be saved; but he who does not believe will be condemned. And these signs will follow those who believe: In My name they will cast out demons; they will speak with new tongues; they will take up serpents; and if they drink anything deadly, it will by no means hurt them; they will lay hands on the sick, and they will recover.

Again, the apostolic mandate, also known as the Great Commission, is being declared by God. By these words He sends His apostles to the ends of the earth. Again the assignment is to multiply by the preaching of the Word to all people and make them disciples. Again we need to take dominion and subdue spiritual wickedness in the heavenlies, powers, principalities, and rulers of the air. And again we are supposed to go out to speak and prophesy identity and purpose to a world that is lost.

Once we are born again and come to an accurate understanding of God's purposes for us, we can touch in the realm of the spirit the power of this spoken assignment that God gives to His people. This mandate stays active in the spirit realm and it will only come to rest once it is fulfilled. This spiritual activity pushes us and creation towards the restoration of all things. Once we experience the reality of this tremendous power we can do nothing but yield to that powerful river of God's Spirit that will bring us to the four corners of the earth.

A river of living water will spring forth from our innermost being (John 4:14) and with a clear focus we will establish God's kingdom wherever we go. With an understanding of the authority given to us, we will subdue darkness to the government of Jesus Christ. The sick will be healed and the dead will be raised! The presence of God will become stronger and stronger as we come closer to the fulfillment of His purposes.

Chapter 2

APOSTOLIC REFORMATION

· ·

DENOMINATIONS AND REFORMATION

When God poured out His Spirit on the day of Pentecost, the New Testament church was called to life. The apostles went into the "known world" of that time and preached the gospel of the kingdom. When we study church history, we notice that after a few generations, despite the increase of believers that were added to the church, deterioration occurred on a certain level. Christianity had become an established faith in the world, but had somehow lost some of its power, anointing, revelation, and sound doctrine. This trend continued throughout the Middle Ages, when faith in Jesus Christ and access to heaven was nothing more than something one could buy. This was why the established Catholic order of that day didn't know much activity of the Spirit. From then on God started to restore certain lost treasures to the church.

Through people like Martin Luther, Charles Finney, John Wesley, William Seymour, Evan Roberts, William Branham,

Kathryn Kuhlman, and many others, God restored essential truths to His church. Through these different restoration moves of the Spirit, different denominations were established. Some of them are what we refer to today as Reformed, Baptist, Evangelical, Methodist, Lutheran, Pentecostal and Charismatic groupings. God's Spirit continually moves forward without stopping. The one problem of denominational Christianity is that it can establish itself immovably around a restoration move of God. Let me explain this a little more.

Every denomination started with a powerful move of God's Spirit that added to the church, but after a few generations most of these groups of people settled themselves for good around that specific move. But we should never ever get settled in a way that we are not able to move again; we should always expect and stretch out for a fresh new move of God's Spirit that will push us deeper into the fulfillment of His plans.

God has promised a land of milk and honey—that is our destiny. We are in Egypt, and the way to our destiny is through the desert. In order to survive the desert, God leads us to different oases. These oases can be compared with the moves of God throughout history. They strengthen us, refresh us, and bring us closer to our ultimate destination. It is the cloud of God's Spirit that guides us from one oasis to another until we reach the Jordan river. But an oasis is not our destiny, rather it is a way to reach our destiny. Most denominations are groups of people that were at one point led by the Holy Spirit to come to a particular oasis. They were privileged to participate in a powerful move of God, but because they didn't have an accurate understanding of the long-term destiny of the church they decided to settle down around that oasis. Even when the cloud of God moved on, they chose to stay in that place of "glory." They confused the move of God with His ultimate purpose for the church.

Once this happens it will only be a matter of time before the well in the oasis will dry out. Throughout the years, God has restored truths such as salvation by faith, a holy lifestyle, the baptism in the Holy Spirit, the gifts of the Spirit, the office of the evangelist, and the office of the prophet. I believe that the one point on God's agenda for today is the restoration of the office of the apostle. We are in the middle of a process which we might call apostolic reformation. Reformation might be a confusing term for some people. What is it, exactly? Simply put, reformation changes mindsets and brings revelation concerning the new move of God. Every move of God starts with reformation. That reformation has the ability to reform the people within the religious established order, so that they become usable in the next move of God. In the coming chapters we'll take a closer look at a few dynamics of reformation.

EGYPTIAN SLAVERY AND BABYLONIAN EXILE

As long as the earth remains, Satan will always try to bring God's people into bondage. Satan knows that as long as the church is submitted to his authority, the purposes of God cannot be fulfilled. People in bondage are unable to participate in the outworking of God's plan.

In the Old Testament, the enemy mainly used two tactics to accomplish his wicked intentions of bringing God's people into a place of slavery. The first form of bondage I will call "Babylonian exile." When the Israelites went astray and started serving other gods, they were taken captive and were forced into exile under Babylonian oppression. The cause of this bondage was lawlessness and disobedience.

The second form of bondage caused by Satan I will call "Egyptian slavery." It is when Satan sees God's people rapidly prosper and multiply, thus becoming a threat to him. So, as in Egypt, Satan will try to come and oppress. His intent is to make slaves. It is interesting to see which tactics he used to keep Israel in bondage. One of the things Pharaoh did was that he gave the instruction that all male babies must be killed. By this act, Pharaoh was working on his long-term strategy to keep Israel in bondage. By killing the male babies he took away the ability to wage war against the Egyptians. This caused Israel to be in a situation that was "hopeless." It is interesting to see that one of the functions of the office of the apostle is to lead the church in spiritual warfare. In other words, if there is no apostolic anointing released in the church, then the ability to wage war will be missing. In Ephesians 6:11-12, Paul the apostle instructs the church of Corinth on engaging in spiritual warfare. The cause of this Egyptian slavery was the opposite of the Babylonian bondage. The thing that triggered Pharaoh's decision to take action against the Israelites was that they were successful, multiplying, growing stronger.

So as one type of bondage is caused by disobedience, the other is caused by success. It doesn't really matter what the cause of bondage is. In both cases the enemy is in authority. In both cases the people of God are unable to emerge in the earth. In both cases the oppression needs to be confronted and broken so God's people can walk in freedom and victory again.

In the Old Testament, Babylon and Egypt were natural places. There was a physical distance between these two locations and their land of promise. Under the new covenant we recognize Babylon and Egypt as symbolic places in the spirit where the church lives in bondage. Satan will always try and rule over the church of Jesus Christ. It doesn't really matter to him how he accomplishes this goal, as long as he can cause the body of Christ to be ineffective. Whenever the church prospers, Satan will try to bind her in religion, tradition and legalism.

He will try and take away spiritual authority so he can do whatever he wants without fear of opposition. Whenever the church begins serving other gods and begins degrading the one true God to a second, third or even lower place, Satan will bring the body of Christ to a place of "Babylonian exile" because of their lawlessness.

Many churches are spiritually stuck in either "Babylon" or in "Egypt." They have lost their identity, purpose, and ability to reproduce. Some of these churches know in their hearts that they are not walking in destiny. They know they need to advance the kingdom of God. They know the Word of God, and they know the Great Commission. Many of these Christians are even sincere and zealous for God; they just don't know how to break free. Some of them do not even know that they are in bondage. The problem is, as long as they are spiritually in Egypt and Babylon, then all they are building are Egyptian pyramids and Babylonian houses. With all their religious activity they display a wrong image of God in the earth. All the effort, energy, and money they invest is used for the fortification of the kingdom of the enemy. As Babylon expands her territory and as Egypt grows stronger through the hands of God's people, the city of Jerusalem lays waste. Christians, who do not realize that they are in a place of bondage, point to Egypt or Babylon and say: "Behold, this is Christianity!"

In order for the church to be able to build effectively, there needs to be a migration to a new position in the Spirit. The land promised to Israel was Canaan, and the city that needed to be rebuilt was Jerusalem. In order to even start building in both the time of Moses and that of Ezra, they first had to physically move to the location of destiny. In the time of Ezra, Jerusalem was the city where the kingdom of God became visible in the earth. Under the new covenant, Jerusalem symbolizes a spiritual position that we need to take. We can only be effective for the kingdom of God when we first migrate to this new position in the Spirit. We need to leave behind Egypt and Babylon, and position ourselves in the land of destiny in order to rebuild Jerusalem, the city of David. This transition in the spirit is the reformation process we need to go through in order to be successful.

Reformation is a process. It will cost time; just like it cost Ezra time to travel from Babylon to Jerusalem, so it will take us time to accurately position ourselves in the Spirit. This migration process is not always easy to measure because it is a spiritual process that is not determined by months, years, miles, and yards. Although we can receive the revelation that we need to be reformed, that doesn't mean that we will be instantaneously reformed. Of course, it is very easy to determine in the natural realm who lives where in the world. Spiritually it is a little different. In one church there can be someone in "Egypt," someone in "Babylon," and someone in "Jerusalem," all sitting in the same row of chairs. Outwardly they look the same, but spiritually two are living in bondage and the other is living in destiny. Because of this we need to take sufficient time to personally go through apostolic reformation, so that we can be sure to build effectively with the anointing that God is releasing in our generation.

MINDSETS AND MENTALITIES

Reformation primarily takes place in our minds. It happens in our thinking. Mindsets and mentalities have to change in order to be effective in the season of God. With every move of the Spirit we need to adjust our mindsets. The reason for this is that with every movement, God restores or adds something to the church that wasn't there before. Within each movement there is an increase of resources and anointing that becomes available to us. As we study the migration from Egypt, as well as from Babylon, we notice something interesting. In Ezra 1: 7-11 we read the following:

King Cyrus also brought out the articles of the house of the Lord, which Nebuchadnezzar had taken from Jerusalem and put in the temple of his gods; and Cyrus king of Persia brought them out by the hand of Mithredath the treasurer, and counted them out to Sheshbazzar the prince of Judah. This is the number of them: thirty gold platters, one thousand silver platters, twenty-nine knives, thirty gold basins, four hundred and ten silver basins of a similar kind, and one thousand other articles. All the articles of gold and silver were five thousand four hundred. All these Sheshbazzar took with the captives who were brought from Babylon to Jerusalem.

The moment the people of God set their minds on leaving Babylon, a certain reaction was created. Articles of silver and gold that belonged to the house of the Lord in the past had been taken by the Babylonians, who placed them in the temples of their false gods. The moment the Israelites arose and decided to leave their place of captivity, those stolen treasures were restored to them. A similar thing happened in the time of Moses, when God's people decided to pursue their destiny instead of expanding the cities of Egypt. The Egyptians restored the treasures and wealth to the people of Israel.

We read about this in Exodus 12: 36:

Now the children of Israel had done according to the word of Moses, and they had asked from the Egyptians articles of silver, articles of gold, and clothing. And the Lord had given the people favor in the sight of the Egyptians, so that they granted them what they requested. Thus they plundered the Egyptians.

We see the same principle working whenever a group of Christians, led by the Holy Spirit, have removed themselves from the established, religious order. They stretched out for more of God's Spirit because they were no longer satisfied with the spiritual state they were in. The moment they decided that they didn't want to live in a place of bondage and restriction, spiritual treasures were released. These treasures represent truth, revelation, and anointing that once belonged to the church but that were taken captive by the domain of darkness.

With every restoration movement the church needs to realign herself with the revelation that is currently being released. This requires an adjustment in our behavior patterns because, now that we have a more accurate understanding about the things of God than before, we'll need to start acting differently. We call the revelation that God gives in a restoration move "present truth." Yet "present truth" changes throughout time as revelation progresses. Every reformation movement brings an increase of "present truth." This requires the church to continually align herself with the "present truth" as each reformation progresses. Christians who are aware of this and who walk on the frontline of this spiritual process are located in the epicenter of the activity of the Spirit.

DELIVERED SPIRITS, BUT AN OPPRESSED MIND

Salvation and reformation are two totally different things. That is why we can never say that "Egyptian" and "Babylonian" Christians are not saved. The established order often comprises zealous and passionate people that have committed their lives with good intentions to Jesus Christ. The Bible teaches us that whoever believes in his heart that Jesus rose from the dead, and confesses with his mouth that He is Lord, that he will be saved (Rom. 10:9). There are many people that meet both conditions, and they are not only "present-truth Christians." The problem is that salvation is not an assurance for freedom!

The difference is that salvation takes place in your spirit, while reformation takes place in your mind. Salvation or "rebirth" enables us to see the kingdom of God, but reformation enables us to enter it(Matt. 16:19). Seeing the kingdom might bring a feeling of awe and wonder, but everything remains untouchable.

Only once we enter the kingdom of God do we have access to its resources and its wealth, and only than can we actually touch it. Only when we enter can we take those treasures of the kingdom and manifest them in the natural realm. That's why the religious order takes away the key of knowledge. By taking it away, we are no longer able to enter the realm of the spirit that is called "kingdom of God" (Luke 11:50).

It is knowledge that opens the door for us. Knowledge is located in the mind, not in the spirit. In Romans 12:2 we read:

And do not be conformed to this world, but be transformed (reformed) by the renewing of your mind, that you may prove what is that good and acceptable and perfect will of God.

2 Corinthians 10:5 puts it this way:

...casting down arguments and every high thing that exalts itself against the knowledge of God, bringing every thought into captivity to the obedience of Christ.

To be able to change the world around us, a transformation first needs to take place in our mind. This transformation enables every blessing that God has released in our spirits to find its way through our minds, through our bodies, and into the world. In other words, our mindset needs to be synchronized with the revelation that God releases in our spirits in order for us live a life of victory and dominion.

When this transformation doesn't happen, Christians are saved by the liberation of their spirits, but unfortunately because their minds are not renewed they still live under the oppression of the enemy. Their daily lives remain unchanged. They do not live in victory. They have the same problems as before. The image of God being portrayed through such a life doesn't appeal to the world that is lost. No one is attracted to a God that is "unable" to change lives. Yet all the while God has prepared a place of freedom and victory.

Reformation happens when we align our minds with the present truth revelation that God releases in our spirits. This alignment causes us to adjust our opinions, change our mindsets, and approach situations with a different mentality. By adjusting our behavior patterns in such a way, we are enabled to take the right place in the spirit, which allows us to effectively build the kingdom of God.

Chapter Three

JOHN THE BAPTIST

THE BRIDGE TOWARDS A NEW ORDER

The life and ministry of John the Baptist can be seen as a blueprint creating a clearer understanding of reformation. Before we cover some of the practical impacts of apostolic reformation on the church, though, let us first look at some basic principles of what reformation really is.

We've seen that reformation enables us to accurately position ourselves within the seasons of God. Reformation is the process that transitions us from the old order of men to the new divine order that God wants to establish: it functions as a bridge, taking us from one place to another. The ministry of John the Baptist had a similar function. The established order of the Old Covenant during his life was about to be fulfilled through the life and sacrifice of Jesus Christ. It was John's function and calling to bring the people of Israel from the old order into the new order of God. John's ministry brought the understanding of what God was about to do in their generation. He prepared the way for the coming of the kingdom. Everyone who submitted themselves to his ministry was prepared to receive God's visitation upon them. Let's take a look at some characteristics of the life of John the Baptist that will give us more insight in the dynamics of reformation.

RIGHTEOUS LEADERSHIP

The first principle of reformation is revealed when we study the history of Zachariah, John the Baptist's father, in Luke 1. We read about the appearance of an angel who announces the birth of a son to Zachariah and his wife Elizabeth. In Luke 1:5-6 we read a report about Zechariah:

> *There was in the days of Herod, the king of Judea, a certain priest named Zachariah, of the division of Abijah. His wife was of the daughters of Aaron, and her name was Elizabeth. And they were both righteous before God, walking in all the commandments and ordinances of the Lord blameless.*

This portion of Scripture describes the environment in which John the Baptist was born. Zachariah was a leader and a priest in the house of the Lord. His wife, Elizabeth, was also born of a lineage of priests, as one of the daughters of Aaron.

We could say that this couple was in active ministry, as Zachariah served in the temple (verse 8). Then we also read that they were both righteous before God, and that they were blameless in all the commandments and ordinances of the Lord. They were not only hard-working and zealous, but they were also righteous and blameless.

This kind of environment will attract the revelation of God. The cradle of reformation is therefore always found in a place where God can trust His leadership to nurture the fresh revelation and bring it to maturity.

THE BARREN PLACE

In Luke 1:7 we read the following:

> *But they had no child, because Elizabeth was barren, and they were both well advanced in years.*

John the Baptist was born in a place that was barren. It wasn't only a barren place, but it was also a hopeless place, as both of his parents were well advanced in years. In the natural it was impossible for them to give birth to a son. Yet it is in that very dry and barren place that God did a new thing. It is in the place of hopelessness that God will make a road in the wilderness. It is in a place without a future where God declares His promise of hope. Reformation will not only come to a place that needs it, but also to a people that acknowledges their need for change and are desperate for it. Reformation comes to a people who realize that if God doesn't do anything, there will be no life in the future.

UNBELIEF MAKES MUTE

After the angel Gabriel spoke concerning the promise of the child, Zachariah stood in unbelief. Instead of receiving the word of the Lord he was led by his circumstances (verse 18). In verses 19-20 we read how the Gabriel responded to Zachariah:

And the angel answered and said to him, "I am Gabriel, who stands in the presence of God, and was sent to speak to you and bring you these glad tidings. But behold, you will be mute and not able to speak until the day these things take place, because you did not believe my words which will be fulfilled in their own."

Zachariah's unbelief caused him to become mute. He was not able to speak anymore until the promise he'd rejected was fulfilled. From this portion of Scripture we can learn a few things. We see how God wants us to receive His word in faith. We will notice that a people who do not receive the revelation of God by faith will become spiritually mute.

This spiritual muteness will cause the message of the man of God to become impotent. Although he may be behind the pulpit trying to declare his message, his words will fall to the ground. The message will be powerless because there is no spiritual substance to it.

The message that was effective and dynamic yesterday is without effect today. Only when we align ourselves again with the present-truth revelation of God will we once again be able to produce a clear sound in the spirit. It was only when Zachariah came in line with the promise of God, by writing down the name of the child, that he was able to open his mouth again and speak (verse 64).

HIS NAME IS JOHN

In Isaiah 43:18-19 we read:

Do not remember the former things, nor consider the things of old. Behold, I will do a new thing, now it shall spring forth; shall you not know it? I will even make a road in the wilderness and rivers in the desert.

God is doing something new. This scripture is teaching us that, in order to know the new thing God is doing, we must first forget the former things. It is very important for us to realize this principle. Old methods, old strategies, old structures will not work anymore.

Even some methods that were initiated by God will have lost their full potency. The strategies of yesterday were effective within the time frame and cultural context of then. But as time proceeds and culture changes, the methods that were a blessing to us yesterday, become our limitation today. If we try to take the structures and strategies of yesterday with us into the new season of God we will notice that this "old wineskin,"— otherwise known as the old church structure—cannot bear the new wine of God's Spirit. We read about the importance of putting new wine into new wineskins in Matthew 9:17:

Nor do they put new wine into old wineskins, or else the wineskins break, the wine is spilled, and the wineskins are ruined. But they put new wine into new wineskins, and both are preserved.

Forgetting the former things of old (the old wineskins) is essential if we want to fully receive the new thing that God is doing in our generation. Please note: this new thing will not only be different, it will also be new! It is nowhere to be found in the past.

The birth of John the Baptist is one clear example of a people willing to forget the former things, or the customary ways of man, in order to embrace the "new thing" of God. The very moment that John the Baptist was born, his mother declared what his name would be. We read about it in Luke 1:59-61:

So it was, on the eighth day, that they came to circumcise the child; and they would have called him by the name of his father, Zachariah. His mother answered and said, 'No; he shall be called John.' But they said to her, 'There is no one among your relatives who is called by this name.'"

In those days it was customary to name your first-born son after his father. A person's name speaks about their identity. In a normal situation, the identity of a first-born child was determined by the identity of his father. In other words, the identity of the past determined the future. This was why the people made the remark, "There is no one among your relatives who is called by this name."

As you can see, reformation brings us something new! This new thing that God is doing in our generation will not compare to anything we have already seen in the past. There will be no point of reference in history. The move that God is releasing in the earth today will go far beyond the moves of yesterday. It is bigger, more powerful, and will establish His divine government in the nations. His name will be John!

JOHN PREACHES IN THE WILDERNESS

Mark 1:2-4:

'Behold, I send My messenger before Your face, Who will prepare Your way before You.' The voice of one crying in the wilderness: 'Prepare the way of the Lord; Make His paths straight.' John came baptizing in the wilderness and preaching a baptism of repentance for the remission of sins."

It is interesting to notice that John's ministry took place in the wilderness. The wilderness or desert is a place without much life and fruit. Yet under the right circumstances, this dry and "hopeless" place appears to be a very fruitful place that can prosper and be a blessing to many. Reformation sees the potential of spiritually dry places and changes the spiritual environment, causing the land to become fruitful once again.

REFORMATION REVEALS THE TRUE SPIRITUAL STATE OF THE CHURCH

From time to time we see that the church has the tendency to elevate cultural preferences and practices to a place where they are misunderstood to be the standard of God. John didn't conform to the cultural religious trends of his day, but instead challenged it by his ministry. We read about this in Matthew 3:4:

And John himself was clothed in camel's hair, with a leather belt around his waist; and his food was locusts and wild honey.

John's appearance wasn't really in line with the established dress code of the day. On the contrary, the religious order paraded around in nice robes (Luke 20:46). At that time, the way people dressed would identify them as an important member of the religious leadership. This emphasis on outward appearance became the primary focus of the scribes and Pharisees, and was turned into a man-made law that was, in turn, placed upon every religious leader.

However, we have to understand that there is nothing wrong with having a dress code or with having cultural preferences. The problem had little to do with the nice robes. The problem was located in the hearts of those religious leaders. It wasn't sinful for them to wear nice clothes, but it became a sin when they put more emphasis on the outward cultural things than on the unseen attitudes of the heart. They were more concerned with how they looked on the outside than how they were on the inside. The moment this happens your robes will turn into an idol that will need to be dealt with.

Culture or outward appearance can cover up the true spiritual state of a church. John challenged this established culture by dressing opposite to what was expected of a religious leader. His intention was not to communicate a message that said the religious order shouldn't wear nice robes, nor was he trying to introduce a new style of fashion. His dressing in a camel-hair coat actually had nothing to do with addressing how people should dress.

He understood that the religious problems didn't have anything to do with outward appearance. The only thing John wanted to accomplish by dressing this way was to challenge the true spiritual state of the people. By dressing this way, he took away the emphasis on the less important things (outward appearance), forcing the people to look on a deeper level. Through this process he helped the people realize that under the cover-up of their beautiful robes was a spiritual wilderness. John was basically showing a true reflection of their spiritual state.

Reformation has a similar effect to John the Baptist's challenge. Reformation always focuses on the spiritual standard, never on the natural. Therefore we should never judge a person by their outward appearance. I have seen many Christians who judge ministers because, in their opinion, they drive too big of a car or live in a house that is too nice. However, the problem has little to do with a person's material possessions. True importance is what's on the inside of a person. Someone who is worried about the natural state of a person has the wrong focus.

We shouldn't be concerned about the question of whether or not someone's car is too luxurious for them but rather about their spiritual state. Once we look at someone through the eyes of the Spirit, we may discover that the reason someone has a big house or a nice car is because of the blessing of God. After all, it is biblical that a righteous life attracts blessing. The key is this: anything, whether cultural or material, that is given more emphasis than the spiritual standard of God will always be challenged by reformation.

Understand me well. I am not saying that outward expression

is not important; I would even go so far as to say that it is very important. I believe that the way someone dresses is a reflection of who they are. It's an expression of character and personality. My point is that the primary emphasis must be on spiritual things and on building the kingdom of God. Our spiritual state will not improve by simply dressing up the outer man. But I do believe that as we are spiritually impacted, our outward appearance will be affected. We read about this principle in Luke 8. Notice the outward change that takes place between verses 27 and 35:

Verse 27: *And when He stepped out on the land, there met Him a certain man from the city who had demons for a long time. And he wore no clothes, nor did he live in a house but in the tombs.*

Verse 35: *Then they went out to see what had happened, and came to Jesus, and found the man from whom the demons had departed, sitting at the feet of Jesus, clothed and in his right mind. And they were afraid.*

It is interesting to note that before this man was spiritually impacted and delivered from evil spirits, he wasn't wearing any clothes. Then after his experience with Jesus, his natural reaction was to immediately clothe himself. I strongly believe that when we choose to focus on the things of God first, only then will we find our true identity. The natural result will then be that we will clothe ourselves to fit our God-given identity. Reformation places a spiritual standard that will ultimately have an effect in the natural realm. Once this happens in its proper order, whatever we see in the natural will reflect what is there in the spirit.

PULLING DOWN RELIGIOUS STRONGHOLDS

Matthew 3:7-9:

But when he saw many of the Pharisees and Sadducees coming to his baptism, he said to them, 'Brood of vipers! Who warned you to flee from the wrath to come? Therefore bear fruits worthy of repentance, and do not think to say to your-

selves, "We have Abraham as our father." For I say to you that God is able to raise up children to Abraham from these stones.'

I used to think that the influence of worldly spirits on the church was far more destructive than the influence of religious spirits. Of course neither one of them should be allowed to infiltrate the church. Yet I've come to the realization that the demonic religious influence is far more evil than it appears to be.

John the Baptist had come to that same conclusion, and therefore committed a lot of his life to pulling down religious strongholds. He was aggressive in dealing with the religious order of the day. To make his point, he even called the Pharisees and Sadducees a "brood of vipers!" We need to understand that the core activity of worldly spirits is to keep people away from Jesus. The assignment of a religious spirit goes far beyond that. Religious spirits don't want to create a gap between Jesus and the church, but instead want to use the church to attack and kill Jesus. Religion uses the very Word of God to crucify Jesus. Religion wants to use the church to drain every drop of life out of her. Religion is the primary cause of spiritual dryness.

Like John, reformation is not afraid to confront the religious order. Reformation calls for repentance. Reformation isn't afraid to say things as they are. Reformation not only confronts religion, but exposes it. It challenges and changes religious mindsets. Religion justifies itself by looking back and boasting in its roots, by saying "we have Abraham as our father." This is the same way many Christians still boast about the glory days of past revivals, without acknowledging the spiritual drought they are in today. Yes, we need to honor our spiritual fathers, but we should not boast in them. They ushered in the move of God in their lifetime and we honor them for that, but it was their glory and not ours. We have our own assignment and there is nothing to boast about until we have accomplished the works that He has prepared for our generation.

DIVINE SEPARATION

Matthew 4:10 speaks about the separation that reformation brings to the church:

And even now the ax is laid to the root of the trees. Therefore every tree which does not bear good fruit is cut down and thrown into the fire.

Reformation is like an ax that brings separation of the fruitful trees from the trees that are not bearing fruit. The fruitful trees are being preserved and the unfruitful trees are being judged by fire. Reformation will judge the church. It will separate the useful from the useless, the good from the bad. Separation is good! Most people associate separation with something negative, but it is actually something that God initiates. We read about this in Hebrews 4:12:

For the word of God is living and powerful, and sharper than any two-edged sword, piercing (separating) even to the division of soul and spirit, and of joints and marrow, and is a discerner of the thoughts and intents of the heart.

Separation, bringing division, is the very nature of the Word of God. The Word is a discerner of the thoughts and intents of the heart. Of course we do not use this sword literally, because our warfare is not against flesh and blood. What we are fighting against are the demonic forces in the heavenlies. Unfortunately, if some people are unwilling to let go of the devils that are tormenting them, even after they are exposed, they are than separated from the body of Christ, together with the devils influencing them. When this happens with more than one person at the same time it could end up in a church split. However, we also see that, because reformation functions as an ax, those who are not willing to submit to what God is doing will be cut off. Therefore we can conclude that some divisions are initiated by God, not for the purpose of separation but for the purpose of growth.

REFORMATION IS NOT THE END GOAL

Reformation is not a goal in itself. As we established in the previous chapters, reformation is a process that functions as a bridge allowing us to cross from an old, established order into the new order of God. This must be a clear part of our message. The fact that we preach a reformation message doesn't mean that we have already arrived, but rather that we are preparing a way to fully transition into the new things of God. John the Baptist was fully aware of this principle, and therefore continuously pointed ahead to what was yet to come. His message prepared the hearts of the people. We read concerning the ministry of John in Matthew 3:3:

For this is he who was spoken of by the prophet Isaiah, saying: 'The voice of one crying in the wilderness: 'Prepare the way of the Lord; Make His paths straight.''

This verse clearly shows that John had an accurate understanding of his role as a reformer. He was only the one who prepared the way, who built a bridge for the people to cross over and meet the Christ.

It was after this reformation message, after the bridge was built, that the Lord could reveal Himself as the Messiah. John the Baptist points this out in Matthew 3:11:

I indeed baptize you with water unto repentance, but He who is coming after me is mightier than I, whose sandals I am not worthy to carry. He will baptize you with the Holy Spirit and fire.

Reformation always points to "He who is coming after me." Reformation always looks ahead and places itself in the shadow of what is about to come. It always makes people aware of the fact that there is something bigger, better, and mightier coming. Reformation simply brings a message to the church. The real power is found in the move of God that follows. Apostolic reformation is not only meant to touch the people of God, but to find its way outside the four walls of the church and into our communities, cities, and nations, causing them, too, to be changed by the power of the living God.

MAKING THE TRANSITION

If it is true that reformation leads us to something better, then there needs to be a time where we stop preaching reformation and actually transition into the new move of God.

It is up to us to recognize the moment. If we do not recognize it and continue preaching the same message too long, we might miss our season and become slaves of our own message. This happened to the children of Israel after Joseph had become the right-hand man to Pharaoh, and they had left their homes to settle in Egypt.

Because God knew there would be a famine in the Promised Land, He had sent Joseph ahead of his brothers to prepare a way of escape. Originally, Egypt was meant to be a temporary place of provision given by God. But when they stayed in that God-given season too long, the place designed by God to be a blessing began to rule over them, forcing them to become slaves.

This principle is always true in relation to reformation, which is meant to be a similarly temporary season. Whenever we stay too long in a God-given season, it begins to rule over us and we become its slave.

However, when the moment of transition comes and we respond to it correctly, our focus will change and we'll transition from proclamation into manifestation. John the Baptist gathered the people, but He who came after, Jesus Christ, sent them into the world.

This is the very nature of the apostolic reformation the church is currently going through. It is gathering Christians who want to align themselves with present-truth revelation of God, that they may become a new frontline of warriors in His army. But the full manifestation of the apostolic anointing that will be released after their response will be what propels these empowered men and women of God into the four corners of the earth. To illustrate this transition more clearly, let's take a look at the words found in John 1:29:

The next day John saw Jesus coming toward him, and said, 'Behold! The Lamb of God who takes away the sin of the world!'

The transition we're talking about takes place the moment John's ministry came to its fullness, therefore launching Jesus' ministry. The verse above describes the moment in history in which this took place.

The moment that John declared "Behold the Lamb of God who takes away the sin of the world!" something happened in the spirit realm. Think about what John just said. Remember that, at that time in biblical history, a lamb represented the sacrifice that was made for the atonement of sin. Throughout the entire Old Testament the people of Israel used this sacrifice and its symbolic act of forgiveness for sins as the center of their religious practices.

With this understanding, we can see why John's message was both revolutionary and controversial. By his declaration, John was identifying Jesus as being "The Lamb of God," the long-awaited Messiah who would take away the sin of the world. In other words, the power that rested upon the Old Testament's system of offering animal sacrifices for the forgiveness of sins was suddenly taken away. The power had lifted from the religious system and was placed upon Jesus Christ, the true Lamb of God! No longer would mankind be forgiven through the sacrificial blood of animals. Now the only way to forgiveness would be through Jesus Christ; He was the one who would take upon Himself the sins of the world once and for all. He was the final sacrifice.

John had accomplished his mission by bringing God's people to this point of transition. Once Jesus was manifested as the Lamb of God, John's ministry, along with his message, changed. Now the focus was on the manifestation of The Lamb. In John 1:35-40, we see something very interesting take place with John's disciples:

Again, the next day, John stood with two of his disciples. And looking at Jesus as He walked, he said, 'Behold the Lamb of God!' The two disciples heard him speak, and they followed Jesus. Then Jesus turned, and seeing them following, said to them, 'What do you seek?' They said to Him, 'Rabbi (which is to say, when translated, Teacher), where are You staying?' He said to them, 'Come and see.' They came and saw where He was staying, and remained with Him that day (now it was about the tenth hour). One of the two who heard John speak, and followed Him, was Andrew, Simon Peter's brother.

Two of John's disciples, who were with him when Jesus came on the scene, must have been listening to John's message, because the moment his ministry came to its fullness, they transitioned into the new order of God. When they heard John declare these words over Jesus, they left him and followed the Lamb of God. Was this a temporary decision? No; "they remained with Him that day." In other words, the moment that the Christ was revealed to these disciples, the ministry of John became invalid. He was no longer necessary for these disciples. John had brought them the one he had been talking about all the time. He had fulfilled his purpose.

Chapter Four

THE RESTORATION OF THE APOSTLE

THE TRIGGER OF THE APOSTOLIC REFORMATION

Before we cover the different areas of impact the current apostolic reformation is having on the church today, I want to take a closer look at one particular restoration that triggered this current reformation: the restoration of the office of the apostle.

THE FIVEFOLD ASCENSION GIFTS

Let us first read Ephesians 4:11:

And He Himself gave some to be apostles, some prophets, some evangelists, and some pastors and teachers, for the equipping of the saints for the work of ministry, for the edifying of the body of Christ.

This well-known scripture talks about how, after He ascended to heaven, Jesus Himself gave these five different gifts to the church in order to equip every saint for the work of the ministry. Notice that the word "some" indicates that only a selected few are called to function as apostles, prophets, evangelists, pastors, and teachers, for the purpose of equipping the saints. Although every believer receives the gift of the Holy Spirit, only a few are given one of the gifts that came from Jesus Himself. In order to be fully equipped for the work of the ministry we need all five of these offices to come into place. The unified formation of this diverse team is called to govern the church. Every one of these five gifts has received a specific grace from Jesus Himself to impart a particular revelation, understanding, and spiritual substance into the body of Christ. Together they form what we call the church government.

Due to the loss of spiritual understanding the church suffered after the first few centuries A.D., most of the offices mentioned disappeared from the scene, causing the church to be governed and equipped by teachers and administrators only. This was the case for centuries long, resulting in an adjustment of dispensational doctrine which taught that, through the death of the early apostles, the post-ascension giftings of apostles, prophets, and evangelists were no longer necessary nor active. Because the church leaders made this decision to adjust their theology according to their circumstances, instead of believing God to bring their circumstances in line with His Word, they placed a limitation upon themselves.

Throughout the last century we have seen major restoration movements that reestablished the office of the pastor and the evangelist. Most churches, for example, feel comfortable using the terms "evangelist," "pastor," and "teacher," to clarify the function of some of their ministers, yet the offices of the prophet and the apostle are not believed to be active today. This way of thinking is a mystery, given that all five of these offices are mentioned in the same verse and are only separated by a comma. It is one thing to have a dispensational mindset, but to separate one verse into different dispensations is absolutely inconsistent theologically. It is even more inconsistent when we take into consideration that the New Testament uses the term apostle at least sixty times more than any of the other four functions mentioned in Ephesians 4:11.

In the 1980s we saw the restoration of the office of the prophet in some Christian circles, but some thirty years later we notice that only a few are comfortable using the term to identify someone who ministers within the sphere of authority that accompanies that gift. Just before the turn of the 21st century we saw a restoration move of God that brought back an understanding and revelation of the office of the apostle, causing the last office of the five-fold team to come into place. This completion of the whole spectrum of the church government team has initiated the reformation we are going through today. Why is it so hard, then, for the majority of the church to accept that apostles and prophets are still meant to function today? Even more, why is it not clear to some that these gifts of Jesus are necessary for the church to become effective and mature?

APOSTLES AND PROPHETS, THE FOUNDATION OF THE CHURCH

I personally believe that the reason it's so difficult for many people to see the importance of apostles and prophets is because of the role they play in establishing the true church. Satan clearly understands that there is tremendous power within the abilities of apostles and prophets once they are released in their right function. He will try anything to keep the apostles and prophets from taking their rightful place. Because of this, there is constant demonic onslaught against the apostolic and prophetic ministry.

One of the most effective strategies in keeping these two post-ascension gifts hidden is to simply make people believe that they are no longer valid for the church. If it is really true that apostles are so important for us today, what role do they play? To answer that question we need to read Ephesians 2:19-22:

Now, therefore, you are no longer strangers and foreigners, but fellow citizens with the saints and members of the household of God, having been built on the foundation of the apos-

tles and prophets, Jesus Christ Himself being the chief cornerstone, in whom the whole building, being joined together, grows into a holy temple in the Lord, in whom you also are being built together for a dwelling place of God in the Spirit.

This scripture gives us a clear description of the Church of Jesus Christ, the household of God, which is the dwelling place for the Holy Spirit. It is compared to a building that is built on the foundation of the "apostles and prophets." As all of us probably know, without a good foundation it is impossible to build a quality house. This portion of scripture reveals to us that, in building the Church, the apostles and prophets are the foundation. Some people will argue this statement by saying that Jesus Christ Himself should be the foundation of the Church, but Ephesians 2 clearly states that apostles and prophets were chosen by God to fulfill this role.

Of course, we understand that Jesus Christ needs to be the foundation of all things, because without Him there wouldn't be a church to begin with. The Word also clearly teaches that Jesus Himself will build His church (Matt. 16:18), and that is true as well. But He also declared that it was to our advantage for Him to go so that the Holy Spirit could come as our Helper (John 16:7). Therefore, by His Spirit, we are strengthened and empowered from on high, able to build and establish the church of Jesus Christ on earth. And Jesus Himself has given apostles and prophets to be the foundation of that church. The Holy Spirit enables those individuals who are called to one of these two offices to become the foundation of the church. And yet it is imperative for us to recognize Him as the "Chief Cornerstone," as the foundation stone that keeps everything together. As He did with Adam and Eve, God has decided to entrust men and women with the great responsibility of establishing His kingdom in the earth and displaying His glory to the nations.

Now, as we understand the vital role of the apostles and prophets in the architectural plan of God in building the church, we can see why there is such warfare against these specific offices. The church can only be built effectively when the foundation is correct. That's why it is so important to come in line with what God is doing today. We also need to remember that, even though the foundation of a building is never visible, what is built on top of it is clearly visible. In the same way, I believe that the current apostolic reformation is laying the foundation for the church to become visible and effective in the earth.

For centuries the church has had the wrong foundation. What we see today is a church with a wrong foundation. As God is restoring the ministry of the apostle a true foundation can be laid. A lot of people believe that apostles are still valid ministers today, but they just add them to the current church structure. However, if we want to build correctly we need to tear down the old building, and lay a new foundation starting from the bottom up. That is why this apostolic reformation has such a tremendous impact on the church as we know it. Everything we know needs to be destroyed before we can start building again. We have to start with the foundation first.

APOSTLES COME FIRST

It's not surprising that in understanding that apostles are a substantial part of the foundation of the church and are meant to be laid first, they are also the first ones in line of the God-appointed ministries given to the church. We read about this in 1 Corinthians 12:28:

> *And God has appointed these in the Church: first apostles, second prophets, third teachers, after that miracles, then gifts of healings, helps, administrations, varieties of tongues.*

Apostles come first. This is not as much of a dictatorial "first" as it is functional. In other words, we could say that apostles have received the grace to be first in authority as opposed to other offices that have received different graces to do other things. Apostles are made to carry responsibility. They are created to lead. They have been given as leaders, as those created to set the church in order.

Their God-given function is to come first in that aspect of

leadership. Throughout the whole New Testament this is confirmed as we discover that the primary leadership of the church at that time consisted of apostles. The word "apostle" is used seventy-four times in the New Testament, as opposed to the words "pastor" and "teacher," which are only mentioned three and fourteen times respectively. The fact that it's used so frequently is just another indication of the importance and weight of responsibility that rests on those who are called to this office. Yet we also see how each God-given office, whether apostle, prophet, teacher, pastor, or evangelist, has its own specific sphere of authority. And as the church matures and is being built upon His intended foundation, each office will come to its God-given place.

THE AUTHORITY OF THE APOSTLE

In order to fulfill this function of being "first," an apostle is given an authority that is above average. This authority will cause people to recognize the apostolic ministry and submit to it. They will do that, not because they are worshiping a man, but because they recognize the God-given gift to the church. They will also understand that Jesus has given this person to them for a reason and that, in submitting to their authority, they can do nothing but benefit. Matthew 10:41 says it this way:

He who receives a prophet in the name of a prophet shall receive a prophet's reward. And he who receives a righteous man in the name of a righteous man shall receive a righteous man's reward.

As we've already discovered, a reward is given to those who receive another in his God-given function. In the same way we receive a prophet or a righteous man, we need to receive the apostle in order to receive the reward that comes with him.

Given the fact that the apostolic ministry is meant to lead, the church was left with a problem before this office began being restored not too many years ago. What do you do when those having the grace to lead are not present or recognized? Many times the problem was momentarily solved by entrusting people with a level of authority for which they didn't have the grace. Often pastors or teachers were given the responsibility to lead the church in a way that only apostle will enable him to work out the clear assignment and orders that he receives from God. A true apostle understands his role, and stays within his God-given sphere of authority. He does not control others by abusing his authority, but instead releases others into their God-given destinies. He will not control other offices like those of pastors and teachers, but will create space and delegate authority, so that they too can function to their fullest potential. Other offices function best when under the leadership of an apostle because that is how they were created to function.

This new apostolic wineskin might give some the impression that apostles are in danger of becoming too independent. Yet a true apostle believes in accountability, humility, and submission. Therefore apostolic networks or churches will seek other apostles to relate to and to be held accountable to. These accountability lines are not written on tablets of stone, or defined by rules and regulations, but are based on friendship and covenant relationships. Because of this, we need to trust God to send the right apostles our way, apostles of character and integrity. Naturally speaking, apostles are servants of all, but in the spirit realm they rule and reign, having no mercy on demonic influence.

As God is restoring the apostolic office to the church, we need to radically adjust our man-made structures that have kept her from advancing in the earth. We will need to give authority to those made to carry leadership responsibilities, the apostles. If we do not transition into this godlier and theologically correct structure, we will discover that the very democratic boards we have created to prevent control and manipulation will actually end up doing the very thing they were intended to prevent.

Of course there will also be false and self-appointed apostles who are "apostles" merely for selfish gain. However, I want to focus more on the genuine apostolic ministry than concentrating on how to recognize the false.

GOING BEYOND THE LOCAL EXPRESSION

There is another paradigm shift that we need to make regarding the ministry of the apostle. Even though we have established that the apostle comes first, and that he needs to carry the primary leadership responsibility for the church, it doesn't mean that those who previously functioned as local pastors should now be replaced by apostles. This is a common mistake, because many people will try to place apostles into the church structure as they've always known it. However, most apostles would probably feel very uncomfortable functioning in a local church setting on a daily base.

Before apostolic reformation there was the local church and that was it. But the ministry of most apostles goes beyond the walls of a "local expression," a term I use instead of "local church" to indicate that an apostolic church is generally bigger than the local church alone. An apostolic church is one that exists out of multiple local expressions. Together they are the church, and together they submit to apostolic authority. This means that there is no need for every local expression to have a local apostle. A local expression could still be led by a pastor. However, this pastor doesn't operate within his own authority, but through the delegated authority received from the apostle he has submitted himself to.

HOW TO DEFINE A TRUE APOSTLE

So what makes an apostle? In studying this subject I came across a definition given by C. Peter Wagner in his book *Spheres of Authority* (Wagner Publications, 2002) which I would like to use. As a "specialist" of the apostolic movement, Wagner suggests the following definition: "An apostle is a Christian leader, gifted, taught, commissioned, and sent by God with the authority to establish the foundational government of the Church within an assigned sphere of ministry by hearing what the Spirit is saying to the Churches and by setting things in order accordingly for the growth and maturity of the Church." This defines the core function of the office of the apostle. Of course every apostle is different. Each apostle will have his unique sphere of authority, as well as his own unique expression and character. Then, around the core activity of the apostle there are other activities, assignments, and areas most apostles function in. For example, most apostles, if not all, leave a trail of supernatural manifestations such as miracles, and signs and wonders. Other areas most apostles function in include establishing doctrine, spiritual fatherhood, leading the church into spiritual warfare, settling disputes, applying discipline, imparting spiritual gifts, and ordering financial distribution. There are many more activities that could be listed, but hopefully these have been enough to underscore the value and the necessity of the restoration of the office of the apostle.

Chapter Five

LEADERSHIP AND AUTHORITY

* *

FROM GROANING TO REJOICING

The Old Testament is filled with historic accounts that prophetically speak about the apostolic mandate that is being picked up by the church today. Accounts of the lives of men such as Joshua and Ezra, as well as the well-known accounts of King David, are merely shadows of the apostolic age that is upon us.

As we take a closer look at the story of Joshua, for example, we recognize a lot of parallels to events today. Joshua was the spiritual, apostolic-type of leader in the Old Testament, who led the people of God into battle to possess the Promised Land. It is a great account and many have been inspired by Joshua's obedience, focus, courage, and determination. In fact, many Christians are so inspired that they are looking for 21st century Joshuas to lead them into victory and into the promises of God for their lives. Yet many of these same Christians have suffered heartache and abuse from spiritual leadership in the past, making it difficult for them to again submit to spiritual authority, especially apostles. This is because a superficial, outward observation of an apostle might remind them of past situations. It is unfortunate that many of us have been confronted with spiritual control and manipulation from our leaders at some point. The wounds of these past abuse situations have caused the spiritual eyes of many to be blinded, making them unable to discern the Joshuas of today.

Those who can identify with this will probably recognize truth in the words found in Proverbs 29:3:

But when a wicked man rules, the people groan.

Those who have experienced corrupt leadership know what it is to groan. They have decided one thing, and that is never to put themselves in that situation again. This is, of course, good and healthy. God doesn't want us to be in a place of groaning, but rather in a place of rejoicing. He wants us to realize that even though we might have encountered a "wicked man" in authority, it doesn't mean that there is no such a thing as righteous leadership. In verse 2 of the same chapter we see the result of righteous leadership: "When the righteous are in authority, the people rejoice."

In this season, the Spirit of God is compelling us to deal with our past hurts, and those things which have caused the eyes of our heart to be blinded, and to stretch out to what lies ahead. When we are willing to respond to this call, the scales that the enemy has placed on our eyes will fall off. This will enable us to discern that, indeed, there is a righteous leadership that God has raised up to lead us into our destinies. God will show us and connect us to the Joshuas and Calebs that do have "a different spirit"(Josh. 14:12), and that do have the mind of Christ. Our groaning will turn into rejoicing, as we willingly decide to submit to this God-given leadership.

ORDER AND CHAOS

A prophetic eye is required if we want to see God's order amidst the chaos of exposed sin and corruption in many Christian leaders and role models over the last decade. Manipulation, control, financial abuse, pedophilia, adultery, divorce, homo-sexuality, quarrels and hate are just a few clear examples of what has been exposed. Many have given up their destinies and decided to pursue secular careers and worldly desires. I have seen just as much sin within the church as I have seen in the world. I know that I am not the only one. Many of us were born into a generation that will go into the history books as an unrighteous generation before God. Seeing this spiritual chaos makes it easy to get confused, disappointed, and bitter. Yet when we discern by the Spirit what is taking place, the cloud of confusion will lift and clarity will be our portion.

Joshua also grew up in a generation that was also character-ized by sin and disobedience. They had wandered aimlessly in the hot wilderness for forty years—the lifespan of a whole gen-eration. In reading this account, we discover that God had a two-fold purpose for their forty-year season of wandering. As we begin to understand these two purposes we will also start to see order in the apparent "chaos" all around us.

The first purpose He had was for a whole generation to per-ish in the wilderness. Just imagine; as you were growing up, all you would see were people around you dying without seeing the fulfillment of God's promises. Your parents, your family members, your leaders, they would all die without having seen the fulfillment of their destinies. One by one, all those who raised you, and those that used to be an example to you, die in the wilderness.

The reason for this was that their generation was full of unbelief and disobedience when the time came to inherit the promise. God responded to their disobedience through judgment. We read the history of these events in Numbers 13 and 14. Let's take a closer look at a specific portion, Numbers 14:20-23 and 28:

> Then the Lord said: 'I have pardoned, according to your word; but truly, as I live, all the earth shall be filled with the glory of the Lord—because all these men who have seen My glory and the signs which I did in Egypt and in the wilder-

ness, and have put Me to the test now these ten times, and have not heeded My voice, they certainly shall not see the land of which I swore to their fathers, nor shall any of those who rejected Me see it.'" "Say to them, 'As I live,' says the Lord, 'just as you have spoken in My hearing, so I will do to you: The carcasses of you who have complained against Me shall fall in this wilderness, all of you who were numbered, according to your entire number, from twenty years old and above.'

Even as God had purposed to judge the entire rebellious generation in their forty years of wandering, we also need to understand that God's second purpose was to raise up a righteous younger generation. The same purpose is true for us. We too have witnessed an entire spiritual generation being judged, yet in the midst of this God is already busy raising up a new, righteous generation. Instead of becoming bitter and frustrated when seeing the corruption of the older generation, we need to recognize that we can be part of the new generation. However, if we do not decide to be a part of the righteous generation, we will die with the rest in the "wilderness," without seeing the promises of God fulfilled in our lives.

UNDER AUTHORITY GIVES AUTHORITY

Submission to God-given authority is a biblical principle. Yet when the eyes of our spirit are blinded by past hurts of spiritual abuse it is difficult to keep things in perspective. Often I have heard disappointed Christians say things like, "I am a believer, but that doesn't mean I need to be part of a church!" Even former church leaders have told me this. Obviously it is possible for someone to come to a place in life where they throw out everything they believed concerning authority. And although it is true that you don't have to be part of a church to be saved, biblical leadership is still essential for a successful Christian walk. In Matthew 8:5-10 we read a clear principle:

Now when Jesus had entered Capernaum, a centurion came to Him, pleading with Him, saying, 'Lord, my servant is lying at home paralyzed, dreadfully tormented.' And Jesus said to him, 'I will come and heal him.' The centurion answered and said, 'Lord, I am not worthy that You should come under my roof. But only speak a word, and my servant will be healed. For I also am a man under authority, having soldiers under me. And I say to this one, "Go," and he goes; and to another, "Come," and he comes; and to my servant, "Do this," and he does it.' When Jesus heard it, He marveled, and said to those who followed, 'Assuredly, I say to you, I have not found such great faith, not even in Israel!'

Jesus marveled when He heard this man speak. The centurion understood the dynamics of authority because he himself was a man under authority. Therefore, because he was under authority, he was given the authority to be in authority over others. This same principle is true for us. We only receive spiritual authority when we submit to God-given authority. Jesus has given apostles as a gift to the church, to function in a place of authority. As we freely submit to this leadership, we then receive the authority to do what we need to do.

GOD CHOOSES THE PEOPLE FIRST

Because I know that some people are afraid of the word authority, I would like to emphasize one of the most important leadership principles. Apostles or other governmental offices need to realize that God always chooses the people first, and then finds a man who can lead them into freedom. Let me explain this more clearly by referring to Exodus 2:23-25:

Now it happened in the process of time that the king of Egypt died. Then the children of Israel groaned because of the bondage, and they cried out; and their cry came up to God because of the bondage. So God heard their groaning, and God remembered His covenant with Abraham, with Isaac, and with Jacob. And God looked upon the children of Israel, and God acknowledged them.

This is a powerful portion of scripture that reveals the heart of God for His people. As we know, the children of God were in bondage, suffering under the oppressive hand of Pharaoh, king of Egypt. God had given them many promises, but instead of seeing them fulfilled they were forced into slavery under the rule of an unrighteous man. Then we read in verse 23 that they cried out because of the bondage. They were in a bad place; they were suffering and there was no way out. The following verses reveal four responses from God to the cry that went up to Him.

1) God heard their groaning

2) God remembered His covenant

3) God looked upon the children of Israel

4) God acknowledged them

These four points give us a clear picture of how God looks at us when we are being oppressed. When we cry out in a place of despair, this is what happens in the heart of God. The last of these points says that "God acknowledged them." God loves His people, and He wants to help them. It is very interesting to see how God made His acknowledgment practical. The way in which He sends help is revealed in the following verses (Ex. 3:1-2 and 9-10):

> *Now Moses was tending the flock of Jethro his father-in-law, the priest of Midian. And he led the flock to the back of the desert, and came to Horeb, the mountain of God. And the Angel of the Lord appeared to him in a flame of fire from the midst of a bush." "(God speaking) Now therefore, behold, the cry of the children of Israel has come to Me, and I have also seen the oppression with which the Egyptians oppress them. Come now, therefore, and I will send you to Pharaoh that you may bring My people, the children of Israel, out of Egypt.*

As a result of God's acknowledgment, He appears to Moses in a flame of fire. He reveals His heart to Moses concerning His children. He repeats the fact that He has heard their cry, and that He has seen their oppression. Then He says, "Come now, therefore, and I will send you to Pharaoh that you may bring My people, the children of Israel, out of Egypt." This is what the apostolic ministry is all about. Moses was sent with clear orders, authority, and mandate to bring God's people into freedom. Notice the order of events. The apostolic call of Moses was a result of the cry of the people. In other words, Moses was called to be there for the people, and to serve them by leading them into freedom. God always chooses the people first.

Once He has chosen the people, He will than find a qualified man or woman who can be entrusted with the authority to lead them. This principle reveals the core function of leadership. God doesn't select leaders as a goal in itself, but more than anything as a means to serve and lead His people into freedom.

If the people of Israel hadn't allowed themselves to be led by Moses, they would have never left Egypt. This shows us how important it is to receive those apostles that God sends. We can never walk in the full destiny that God has prepared for our lives if we do not receive those that He has called to be in authority. Let's read again the scripture about the five governmental offices that Jesus has given to the church, in Ephesians 4:11:

And He Himself gave some to be apostles, some prophets, some evangelists, and some pastors and teachers, for the equipping of the saints for the work of ministry, for the edifying of the body of Christ.

Why did Jesus give us these leaders? For the equipping of the saints for the work of the ministry! Every saint is called to do the work of the ministry. Only when we open ourselves freely to these five governmental offices will we be fully equipped, and the body of Christ will be edified. However, if we choose not to submit to this authority, we will not be equipped and therefore disabled in our ability to minister to others.

COVENANT AND SUBMISSION

One more thing about submission to authority: it should always be voluntary. True submission is never imposed, forced or coerced. Because of this freedom of choice, submission can never be mixed with manipulation. Let's look at it from another angle.

Submission is based on establishing a mutual covenant with another by a declaration of trust. We read about this in 1 Chronicles 12:16-18:

> *Then some of the sons of Benjamin and Judah came to David at the stronghold. And David went out to meet them, and answered and said to them, 'If you have come peaceably to me to help me, my heart will be united with you; but if to betray me to my enemies, since there is no wrong in my hands, may the God of our fathers look and bring judgment.' Then the Spirit came upon Amasai, chief of the captains, and he said: 'We are yours, O David; We are on your side, O son of Jesse! Peace, peace to you, And peace to your helpers! For your God helps you.' So David received them, and made them captains of the troop." These verses illustrate very accurately the covenant I am talking about. These men came to David because they recognized a God-appointed leader. Then, after testing their heart motivation, David shares his desire. He says that if their motivations are good, than he wants to unite his heart with theirs This isn't control, but more than anything it is an example of respect. These men want to submit to David, and he wants to make a covenant with them by uniting their hearts. After declaring trust in David's leadership by saying "We are yours, O David!" he honors them by making them captains of the troop. Again we see a divine principle: submission to God-given authority will only give authority.*

In this current apostolic reformation, the same question is asked of us: Are you for me or are you against me? If we can submit to the apostolic authority that God sends to us by declaring trust in the man of God, than our hearts will be united with him. The result will be a covenant relationship that will allow us to be released into a higher level of God's purpose. The apostolic leadership that God is raising up in our generation is a righteous leadership. It consists of men and women after God's own heart. These leaders have laid down their lives for the sake of the gospel of the kingdom and they live to serve God's people. Even though we may have experienced a wicked ruler in the past, a new day is upon us. The apostolic leadership that God has sent to us today will say the very thing we read in Nehemiah 5:15:

But the former governors who were before me laid burdens on the people, and took from them bread and wine, besides forty shekels of silver. Yes, even their servants bore rule over the people, but I did not do so, because of the fear of God.

Chapter Six

TEAM MINISTRY

. . . .

One of the reasons many people find it difficult to trust leaders is because they do not want history to repeat itself. In today's reformation, God is requiring a pure character and the fear of the Lord to reside in His leaders. It is also noticeable how God is changing the old mentality and upgrading the structure within this new generation of leaders. Let's take a look at the different characteristics of today's leaders.

PLURAL PRIESTHOOD

It is impossible for an individual to display the whole spectrum of the manifold grace of God to the world around us. Even though the fullness of God's Spirit lives in us, it is still impossible to demonstrate every aspect of God's being by ourselves. That is why God has created us as different members of the same body. If we want to reflect an accurate image of who God is we will need to work together as a team. The Word of God teaches us that one will defeat a thousand and two will defeat ten thousand. There is a multiplication of authority when you work together as a team. It is critical that all five of the governmental offices (apostle, prophet, teacher, evangelist, pastor) work together to produce balanced Christians.

Intellectually, most of us embrace the concept of teamwork. But somehow, on a practical, daily level, it seems hard to apply team ministry. It would seem that we lack the revelation on how to keep a clear, end-responsible person in authority while working within a peer-level team. To develop a clear understanding of team ministry, I would like to use two illustrations, the "Moses model" and the "Joshua model." Both need to be applied to today's church, but only the "Joshua model" reflects a clear picture of team ministry on a governmental level. Let's look at both models to see the differences.

The "Moses model" is based on dividing the workload of a ministry. Moses was the one-man leader—a clear picture of how many churches function today. Because he was clearly the one in charge, he was therefore expected to carry all the responsibility that came with being the leader. Everyone who has ever been in a position of authority will probably agree that responsibility in leadership almost always comes with a big workload. Let's read how Moses dealt with this workload as he responded to his father-in-law Jethro in Exodus 18:17-23:

> So Moses' father-in-law said to him, 'The thing that you do is not good. Both you and these people who are with you will surely wear yourselves out. For this thing is too much for you; you are not able to perform it by yourself. Listen now to my voice; I will give you counsel and God will be with you: Stand before God for the people, so that you may bring the difficulties to God. And you shall teach them the statutes and the laws, and show them the way in which they must walk and the work they must do. Moreover you shall select from all the people able men, such as fear God, men of truth, hating covetousness; and place such over them to be rulers of thousands, rulers of hundreds, rulers of fifties, and rulers of tens. And let them judge the people at all times. Then it will be that every great matter they shall bring to you, but every small matter they themselves shall judge. So it will be easier for you, for they will bear the burden with you. If you do this thing, and God so commands you, then you will be able to endure, and all this people will also go to their place in peace.'

This is a clear description of how the "Moses model" works.

Because Moses carried most of the workload by himself his father-in-law said: "you will surely wear yourselves out." The next thing Jethro suggested was to divide the work among a team of leaders on different levels. Although this was wise and necessary, it shouldn't be confused with team ministry on a governmental level. Notice that this portion of scripture also says, "Then it will be that every great matter they shall bring to you, but every small matter they themselves shall judge." As we've just read, the workload was being divided among different levels of leadership in a hierarchical sense.

In other words, Moses was the highest authority and therefore dealt with the great matters, and every small matter was to be judged by the appointed leaders under him. This "Moses model" is not something we should despise. Yet I would like to add a dimension to this way of working by introducing the "Joshua model" of leadership. By understanding both models, our mentality shifts to a new dimension, enabling us to progress further into the purposes of God.

It was Moses, the one-man leader, who brought God's people out of bondage. In the same way the "Moses model" church has brought God's people to a place of freedom. This leadership model will bring the church of Jesus to the "river Jordan," as it gives the people of God a taste of destiny and purpose. Because of their godly purpose, we need to honor the Moses-type leaders— they have brought us to where we are. Yet we also need to understand that, as God then upgrades to a "Joshua model" type of church, the days of Moses are over for good. Yes, it was the one-man Moses who split the waters of the Red Sea and led God's people into freedom. But it was the plural priesthood of Joshua's time that split the waters of the Jordan and led God's people into the Promised Land. Moses was able to lead the people through the wilderness, but Joshua's plural leadership was able to lead the people into destiny.

Let's take a closer look at the structure of this "Joshua model," and discover what it is that will enable us to break the limitations of the "river Jordan" and release us into the fullness of

God's promises. We start by reading Joshua 3:14-17:

So it was, when the people set out from their camp to cross over the Jordan, with the priests bearing the ark of the covenant before the people, and as those who bore the ark came to the Jordan, and the feet of the priests who bore the ark dipped in the edge of the water (for the Jordan overflows all its banks during the whole time of harvest), that the waters which came down from upstream stood still, and rose in a heap very far away at Adam, the city that is beside Zaretan. So the waters that went down into the Sea of the Arabah, the Salt Sea, failed, and were cut off; and the people crossed over opposite Jericho. Then the priests who bore the ark of the covenant of the Lord stood firm on dry ground in the midst of the Jordan; and all Israel crossed over on dry ground, until all the people had crossed completely over the Jordan.

The ark of the covenant represents the manifest presence of God. In the Old Testament, it was the physical location from which God governed His people. The ark was designed to be carried by four priests. When crossing the Jordan, God's government rested on the shoulders of the four Levite priests. This gives us a prophetic picture of a New Testament church government of plural leadership. It should consist of different leaders that function on the same governmental level, as opposed to a shared leadership that is divided over different levels of responsibility.

Before we can inherit God's promise by fulfilling the apostolic mandate, we will see the apostolic church being upgraded to this "plural priesthood" type of leadership. As Joshua 1:2 declares "Moses My servant is dead," the time of one-man church leadership will be over for good. Now is the time for the church to be governed by a plurality in leadership. Whenever the ark of the covenant was being carried by less than four Levites, the government became imbalanced. The same is true for us when we do not walk with the God-given revelation to carry the government of the church among a priesthood of leaders. Now let's look at Joshua 3:1-3:

Then Joshua rose early in the morning; and they set out from Acacia Grove and came to the Jordan, he and all the children of Israel, and lodged there before they crossed over. So it was, after three days, that the officers went through the camp; and they commanded the people, saying, 'When you see the ark of the covenant of the Lord your God, and the priests, the Levites, bearing it, then you shall set out from your place and go after it.'

Today there is a sound heard in the Spirit saying, "Whenever you see a priesthood of leaders carrying the government of the church on their shoulders, that is the place you need to be! Go after it! It will lead you and release you into your destiny!"

NEITHER DEMOCRACY NOR DICTATORSHIP

The fact that we talk about shared leadership doesn't mean that this team should function on a democratic basis. Democracy in the church is a weapon of the enemy to deceive and make the body of Christ impotent. It is a political structure that cannot be found anywhere in the Bible as a divine government structure for the church. It is Jesus who selects, calls, and places people in governmental positions, not the people. Remember that Ephesians 4:11 says,

And He Himself (Jesus) gave some to be apostles, some prophets, some evangelists, and some pastors and teachers.

It is Jesus, not a majority in the congregation, who chooses His leaders. Democracy causes leaders to become dependent on the people, while the people also become dependent on their leaders. In democracy the majority always leads, while history shows that God often works through a remnant, or in other words a minority. Throughout the Bible we notice that most of the time God uses the minority to fulfill His purposes. If we always let the majority decide what is going to happen, we are in danger of missing out on the plan of God.

Democracy speaks of the spirit of Korah that came against Moses in Numbers 16:1-3: "Now Korah the son of Izhar, the son of Kohath, the son of Levi, with Dathan and Abiram the

sons of Eliab, and On the son of Peleth, sons of Reuben, took men; and they rose up before Moses with some of the children of Israel, two hundred and fifty leaders of the congregation, representatives of the congregation, men of renown. They gathered together against Moses and Aaron, and said to them, 'You take too much upon yourselves, for all the congregation is holy, every one of them, and the Lord is among them. Why then do you exalt yourselves above the assembly of the Lord?'

The accusation of Korah was against Moses' position as a leader. He accused Moses of being a self-appointed leader, and he promoted equality by saying that each one of them was holy. It's true that everyone is equal in a certain sense, but Moses was anything but self-appointed. In fact, God had to come on very strong to make him take his position as leader. Moses had not exalted himself above the rest; God had chosen and appointed him.

Korah's story sounded good and accurate on a certain level, but on another he was guilty of which he was accusing Moses. Korah was the one exalting himself to the level of Moses. Whenever democracy takes over the governmental level of a church you soon begin to see the same dynamics take place. Our God-given leadership will be degraded by the democratic spirit as it tries to stir up the congregation against divine authority. As judgment came upon Korah and his followers, judgment will come upon everyone who comes against God-appointed leadership. When we continue reading the history of Kora in Numbers 16:28-33 we see how this judgment takes place:

And Moses said: 'By this you shall know that the Lord has sent me to do all these works, for I have not done them of my own will. If these men die naturally like all men, or if they are visited by the common fate of all men, then the Lord has not sent me. But if the Lord creates a new thing, and the earth opens its mouth and swallows them up with all that belongs to them, and they go down alive into the pit, then you will understand that these men have rejected the Lord.' Now it came to pass, as he finished speaking all these words, that the ground split apart under them, and the earth opened its mouth and swallowed them up, with their households and all the men with Korah, with all their goods. So they and all those with them went down alive into the pit; the earth closed over them, and they perished from among the assembly.

Different leaders have initiated a counter-movement as a reaction to the democratic spirit that has infiltrated the church. These leaders have changed their leadership culture into a dictatorship.

Because they didn't like one end of the spectrum they became extremists on the other end. Such a dramatic change in structure is a deceiving process that can change you into a controlling leader before you realize. Often, leaders that have the tendency to be controlling have a difficult time discerning and implementing the "Joshua model" of team ministry. What we, as leaders, need to realize is that shared governmental responsibility is neither democratic nor dictatorial. It is theocratic! Theocracy is a divine leadership structure that works under the old, as well as the new, covenant. It is a structure where Jesus Himself is the head of His church. He chooses and appoints leaders, instead of men choosing and appointing leaders. It is a God-governed environment, where He is putting in place church government.

Although the ark of the covenant was carried by four Levites, it is clear that Joshua was still the end-responsible leader. Joshua, as a picture of the apostle, oversaw and instructed the Levites who, as a picture of the other offices, carried the ark. Even though governmental responsibility should be shared among different leaders, there are still functional differences between each of those leaders. There is only one office that is designed to function as end-responsible. In this past example, Joshua was clearly functioning as the apostle.

THEOCRACY IS ROOTED IN EQUALITY WITH A FUNCTIONAL DIFFERENCE

The two extremes of democratic and dictatorial leadership

come as a result of not being able to find the right balance. Yet the Word of God gives a clear understanding concerning these things. As we look at God, we discover a clear balance in the Godhead. When we study how the Father, Son and Holy Spirit relate to one another we discover a very profound leadership principle. As we should all agree, God is three persons. These three persons are God the Father, God the Son and God the Holy Spirit. All three are God, therefore all three are equal on the God level. The Father is God, the Son is God, and the Spirit is God. They are all completely God! And yet all three are different. God the Father sits on the throne. God the Son (Jesus), became a man, walked among us, and paid the price. God the Holy Spirit came to us as Comforter. And even though they are all equally God, they are completely different on a functional level. God the Father didn't die on the cross. The Holy Spirit is not on the throne; He is not even sitting at the right hand of the Father.

In many ways there is a clear, functional difference between the Godhead. And so we see that each function cannot be changed or replaced by another or by another's function. Although they are equal, each one has a functional difference. This point leads us to ask, "Are all Christians equal?" And we can answer in the same way. Yes, we are all sons of the living God—yet on a functional level we are very different. We are one body with many different members. Some are given to be leaders, others are not. Yet all members within the governmental leadership team are equal. They all "carry the ark." On the other hand, only one has the function of being end-responsible. In that sense they are very different.

As we begin to understand these dynamics of leadership, we will be able to work together on one horizontal level and at the same time recognize each individual's functional difference. I'm reminded of a statement I once heard from a successful business man: "There are two things that I notice when I look at successful people.

The first thing is that they all possess excellent qualities that they are using to the fullest. The other thing is that they seek to work with experts who are strong where they are weak. A partnership like this is destined to succeed!"

I believe this wise remark clearly reflects the profound value of team ministry. A responsible leader possesses certain qualities that he needs to use to the fullest. Yet he also needs to realize that in order to succeed he will need to find experts in his areas of weakness. In the same way, the spectrum of ministry needed in order to succeed is broader than the singular anointing of one man of God. For this reason we need to seek partners to join in covenant with, and together we will cross the river Jordan and release God's people into destiny.

Chapter Seven

THE COMPLETION OF CHURCH GOVERNMENT

MANAGING THE GOVERNMENTAL SPECTRUM OF MINISTRY

With the restoration of the apostolic office a dimension is added to the church that we have not seen in recent church history. We have already seen that apostles come first in a functional sense of responsibility and authority. Now we need to look in more detail how this function of being first in authority is absolutely necessary in establishing balanced team ministry on a governmental level. The reason is that the apostolic anointing comes with the grace and ability to oversee, manage, and to unite the whole spectrum of governmental ministry. The apostle has the grace to be able to see how the different types of leadership should relate to each other. He is able to set church leadership in order, and also carries the grace to release each one of the Ephesians 4:11 gifts into their area of expertise.

We've already read how Joshua—who is a picture of the apostolic ministry—distinguished himself from the others in authority by functionally separating himself from the four Levites who carried the ark. By taking this distance he was able to oversee and instruct the other four ministries (the Levites) carrying the government of God (the ark of the covenant). In the same way, the New Testament apostle positions himself so that he is able to oversee and manage the complete spectrum of ministry.

Again, I would emphasize that this distance in the spirit between the apostle and the other four Ephesians 4:11 gifts is not positional, but rather functional. All different types of anointings within church government should submit functionally to the apostolic anointing. In the realm of the spirit the apostle comes first and takes the highest place. An apostle should therefore be end-responsible over a church. Just imagine for a minute that you are on the summit of a mountain. Once you have taken your position on the top you are well able to oversee the geographical area around that mountain. Whether you look to the north, east, south, or west, you have a clear view because you are on the highest place. Once you descend from the mountain to a lower place on a particular side, your view will narrow down to that singular side of the mountain. Even though you are able to see that particular area in more detail, you will lose sight of what is happening on the other side.

This same principle is true for the apostolic ministry. The apostle is supposed to stand on the top of the mountain, which represents his place in the spirit. From there he can clearly oversee all 360 degrees around the mountain, which represents the spectrum of ministry that is necessary to govern the church successfully.

This is a quality or gift that the other four governmental offices do not have, as each is given, made, shaped, and molded to function within its own area of expertise. As long as each office works within its God-given field, it will be effective and powerful.

Those in these offices may even carry insight into the spectrum of ministry that borders their sphere of authority, but they'll lack the ability to oversee and set in order all of the governmental gifts. The grace to work out that particular task has been given to the apostle.

Once we recognize this apostolic grace and submit to it, a space will be created in the realm of the spirit which will enable all other ministries to develop and grow. When an apostle takes his place correctly, all types of anointings, functions, and callings will be cultivated, raised u,p and released. This will allow the body of Christ to properly function as a whole. Because of his "helicopter view," and also his ability to recognize different types of anointing, the apostle is well able to activate every believer in the context of ministry that is right for them. The result will be a church that functions properly and a body that declares a healthy and balanced message.

This whole dynamic of church government explains why the end-responsible leadership of the early church consisted of apostles alone. They governed the early church using Jerusalem asa base. On more specific levels of government, the other were then released and set in order.

UNDERSTANDING PARA CHURCH

There was a point, before the apostolic ministry began to be restored, when the church wasn't able to be governed properly. This was mainly due to the lack of apostles and prophets in the foundation of the church. Because of this, many ministries walked into problems. Because there were no apostles in place, overall responsibility of the church was given to one of the other offices. In most cases this person was referred to as the "pastor" of the church. In reality, these "pastors" were often shepherds, teachers, or evangelists and, in very rare cases, maybe a prophet. But when one of these offices is given the responsibility that only an apostle can accurately carry out, we discover an all-too-familiar dynamic.

When a church is governed by an evangelist, for example,

you'll notice that the people attracted to his ministry are those who are also called to function within that same anointing. Because of this the space that an evangelist creates on his own is limited. It is limited to "his side of the mountain." The negative reality is that someone who is called to function within a different anointing won't find space to grow and develop within that ministry. This limitation will create frustration because his leader will not understand him. Anyone with a different anointing will in all likelihood ultimately leave that particular ministry.

I have known many who did not understand this dynamic. As a result they came to believe that they were different from the rest, and would assume that there was no place for them anywhere. This caused them to continue their walk with God independently. If people did understand this dynamic they would leave the church and try to find another ministry that was able to release them in their gifting. Many times the "pastor" labeled the person who left as rebellious and unwilling to submit to spiritual authority. I have seen this same misunderstanding and poor judgment over and over again. The result is that many churches governed by non-apostles become superficial and narrow-minded. The world then looks at these churches as unbalanced and shallow—and many times that's right!

When the apostolic dimension is not added to a church we also see that spiritual life is often limited to a local church expression, while God has called them to a ministry beyond the local dimension. And yet again we see the same dynamics at work.

The term "parachurch organization" is a result of these dynamics. Most often a parachurch organization is one that should have been part of a church structure, but wasn't able to find its place there because the church was governed by non-apostles.

Many times they were forced—or often even led by the Spirit—to establish themselves as an independent ministry. A parachurch organization is established when a certain person carries a bigger or different anointing than the local church "pastor." For this reason he doesn't find space to nurture and develop his ministry in the local church setting, causing him to leave and start a specific ministry on his own. The result of this is that the body of Christ is chopped up in different, independently specialized segments of ministry. Through this parachurch principle we have seen many ministries develop into independent organizations such as missions organizations, rehab centers, conference centers, Bible schools, counseling institutions, and more. Because these different specialized organizations are mainly on their own, people are often forced to choose where to commit primarily. And all of this is done while each of these ministries reflects and imparts an anointing that should be found under the roof of one house.

In a non-apostolic church structure, parachurch development will automatically be promoted. This is because the ministry of the apostle, which is meant to be creating space for the different ministries in the church, is absent. In this case most people will commit to a local church for the community atmosphere and the social contacts. But to feed their desire for ministry they will leave their local church for several years to attend an independent Bible school. Upon graduation, they'll probably hook up with another missions organization to practice what they have learned. Then, when they need specialized counseling, they will seek help from another organization that is committed to that specific ministry.

Specializing isn't wrong. In fact, it is absolutely necessary. Yet to specialize independently like this will cause the body of Christ to be divided into little pieces of specific ministry. There was a time that parachurch ministries needed to be developed, but with the restoration of the apostle we see that a more effective structure is being built. When the apostolic ministry takes its correct, governmental place, it will create an environment that allows the development of different ministries within the church. This apostolic release will pull the different ministries together and will possess the ability to go beyond local borders. Potential ministries are no longer limited to the anointing of their local leader. But because this local church is only a part of the much broader apostolic structure, there is space to develop beyond the walls of their local expression. They work out their ministry and still are part of the same church.

FUNCTIONAL APOSTLES

As we study the history of different parachurch organizations we discover that many were founded by ministers who were actually called to be apostles but didn't know it. The established church of the day wasn't familiar with the apostolic ministry, and therefore didn't recognize the apostolic anointing. These ministers didn't have much choice but to leave the local church and establish their own independent ministry.

Through this independent ministry they would effectively be able to reach a wide range of different local churches through their specific input.

Let's say we are talking about a person who is called to lead and release many people into the mission field. The local church couldn't carry the weight of such a ministry, so this person starts his parachurch organization. Now he can reach and influence different local churches through his ministry. Through this principle we have seen many huge ministries develop into global organizations. In most of these cases the founders were called to be apostles carrying out a specific mandate of specific ministry. I like to call these types of apostles functional apostles, mandated by God to impart a specific area of ministry.

Apostolic reformation we will ultimately phase out independent parachurch organizations. The fact that they will disappear doesn't mean that there isn't place for functional apostles.

The thing that will change is that these functional leaders will blend into the structure of an apostolic house, and still be dedicated to this specific call reaching numerous local expressions. Instead of functioning apart from the church, these ministries are being integrated as part of the church. This will cause them to reap many benefits.

Chapter Eight

ECONOMICS OF THE APOSTOLIC CHURCH

APOSTOLIC DISTRIBUTION

Another dynamic of the apostolic ministry is that it brings divine order to the economic system of the church. Because the old-order church was chopped up into so many different independent ministries, every part was responsible for raising its own funds. In the same way, most parachurch organizations exist on the gifts of sponsors from different local churches who give on a monthly basis. A lot of energy and time goes into fund-raising activities, which is not necessarily wrong, but it takes away from the real purpose of the organization. By founding a parachurch organization, one places himself in a position of responsibility to raise money for the ministry. I believe there is a higher and more effective order. Someone who is called for a specific ministry shouldn't be burdened with financial tasks unless God has asked that of him. A man or woman of God gifted within a certain office should be able to commit a hundred percent to the work he or she is called to. When someone like this is not part of an apostolic church, their success will be limited by their financial management skills as well as their creativity.

I believe that financial pressures will only increase in parachurch organizations. Why? Because as the apostolic move emerges in the earth, the finances of the church will be greatly affected as it comes into right order, the governmental function of the apostolic anointing. The office of the apostle has the supernatural ability to attract substantial amounts of money. The result will be that independent ministries, which function outside the governmental order of God, will no longer draw from the wealth of the world. The apostolic anointing, on the other hand, will bring a higher, more effective order to the wealth and economics of the church. In establishing this new order of finances, every party involved will benefit and prosper.

Genesis 2:10-12:

Now a river went out of Eden to water the garden, and from there it parted and became four riverheads. The name of the first is Pishon; it is the one which skirts the whole land of Havilah, where there is gold. And the gold of that land is good. Bdellium and the onyx stone are there.

One of the four rivers from Eden was called Pishon. This particular river went throughout the whole of Havilah, a place known for its gold and precious stones. This picture of the river Pishon flowing towards the gold speaks prophetically about the apostolic anointing that brings us to the provision we need to fulfill our mandate. It is the apostolic anointing that will cause us to go to where the finances and blessings are.

Notice that God declares here that the gold He created was good. The righteous desire to have gold or money is a good thing, rather than a bad thing as many people believe. Money is meant to be a tool in the hands of the church to execute God's purposes. The apostolic anointing will not only release financial blessing and favor, but it will also attract finances to the church. This impartation and release of blessing will result in bigger offerings and gifts, which will again add to the wealth of the church. We read in Acts 4:34-37 about the great offerings that were given as a result of the apostle's governmental anointing:

> *...for all who were possessors of lands or houses sold them, and brought the proceeds of the things that were sold, and laid them at the apostles' feet; and they distributed to each as anyone had need. And Joses, who was also named Barnabas by the apostles (which is translated Son of Encouragement), a Levite of the country of Cyprus, having land, sold it, and brought the money and laid it at the apostles' feet.*

We clearly see that the offerings the people brought in the time of apostles' feet.

DEACONS AND DISTRIBUTION

A deacon has the ministry of taking care of social needs, and is also someone with organizational and financial management skills. In the past, many parachurch organizations were focused on social needs and on doing the good work of a "deacon" ministry. In the apostolic church, however, the apostles will be responsible for identifying structural social needs, and for distributing funds to the appointed deacons. In Acts 6:1-6 we find an example of how the apostles were directly involved in this process:

> *...there arose a complaint against the Hebrews by the Hellenists, because their widows were neglected in the daily distribution. Then the twelve summoned the multitude of the disciples and said, 'It is not desirable that we should leave the word of God and serve tables. Therefore, brethren, seek out from among you seven men of good reputation, full of the Holy Spirit and wisdom, whom we may appoint over this business; but we will give ourselves continually to prayer and to the ministry of the word.' And the saying pleased the whole multitude. And they chose Stephen, a man full of faith and the Holy Spirit, and Philip, Prochorus, Nicanor, Timon, Parmenas, and Nicolas, a proselyte from Antioch, whom*

they set before the apostles; and when they had prayed, they laid hands on them.

This account gives us a clear picture of how a healthy church should deal with finances in an effective way. The social need had to do with the neglect of a group of widows, but it could have been any social need. We can apply the principle to be drawn from this passage to different needs such as orphanages, schools, homeless shelters, rehab centers, crisis care, food projects, community development, and more. First, notice that the apostles had the responsibility to see and acknowledge the need that was present.

They also recognized that their primary responsibility was to commit themselves continually to prayer and to the ministry of the word. The next thing they did was to take initiative by calling the congregation together. They declared the need to the congregation, so that everyone present knew about it. This is a crucial moment. As the apostles declared that there was a need to be met they stirred something in the spirit realm. Desires in the hearts of some were awakened by the words of the apostles. The apostles then instructed the congregation to select seven men (functioning as deacons) to take care of the need. After the seven were chosen, the apostles then delegated the responsibility of the project to them. These men were commissioned and released by the laying on of hands by the apostles for their specific task. Through that commission they then received the full authority and all the means they needed to complete the task. This is a clear example of how apostolic distribution can work through the governmental decision of the apostle and the ministry of a deacon.

Unlike governmental leaders and those in the five-fold ministry, deacons are chosen democratically. This tells us something about a deacon's spiritual place. Many churches place deacons on the same line of authority as elders. However, this is incorrect. There's a big difference between the governmental role of an elder and the practical ministry of a deacon. Because of this, leaders need to be careful not to elevate the democratically chosen deacon to the level of the theocratically chosen five-fold gifts of church government. Of course it is possible for God to lead a deacon into one of the five-fold ministry functions, but in such cases there should be a separate acknowledgment of his specific ministry.

Although the ministry of a deacon is not governmental, his effect on society is probably the most underestimated of all ministries. Those who help those in need not only influence people in a tremendous way, but also reveal the kingdom of God. For example, when we compare the deacon ministry with the public ministry of Peter, we notice a remarkable thing. When Peter preached his first sermon on the day of Pentecost, three thousand believers were added to the church because of his message. Obviously this was very powerful. But let's read about the ministry of the deacons after they were released and commissioned by the apostles in Acts 6:6-7:

> ...whom they set before the apostles; and when they had prayed, they laid hands on them. Then the word of God spread, and the number of the disciples multiplied greatly in Jerusalem, and a great many of the priests were obedient to the faith.

Preaching brings the blessing of addition to the church, but the release of the deacons who minister in the social needs of people causes the number of disciples to multiply greatly. Social ministry within the context of the apostolic church will cause the word of God to spread even further, and the church to multiply greatly. Just imagine how much blessing the church can release in the earth by embracing the apostolic move. It will cause the church to become one body that is effective in every area of ministry. As apostles work together with social ministers (deacons), there will be no limits to what God can do through His church.

SPIRITUAL SOCIALISM

Even though apostolic distribution concerning social needs is very necessary, we need to be careful not to change church culture into life. It causes them to remain in a place of bondage and lack. The approach that the church needs to take to social needs should lead people toward a higher standard of living. Our social help, combined with sound doctrine, needs to bring them to a place where they are able to make responsible choices that will propel them in a victorious life of the abundance of God. This way we will not only provide people with short-term relief from social distress, but will also help them in the long-term by equipping them to make the right choices in life. Remember that one of the results of social ministry in Acts 6 was that the word spread. The word needs to be added to our social help in order for it to become effective.

In Luke 15 we read of the prodigal son, who ended up with a tremendous social need. Yet it was his own fault that he ended up eating with the pigs. He made the decision to take his inheritance before his time, and to use it the wrong way. God then led him to a place where he was confronted with the wrong choices he had made. This confrontation led to repentance, which in turn caused him to make responsible decisions again. After he made the right decision to return to his father, blessing was released again; there was a meal for him, a ring for his finger, and a new mantel on his shoulders.

Just imagine for a moment that "Pig Ministries International" had come to visit the prodigal son. Imagine that they had brought him some nice clothes and a decent meal. Do you really think that he would have made the same decision to return to his father's house? I am convinced that he wouldn't have. The social provision they would have given him would have probably kept him from making responsible choices. Now, don't get me wrong, social ministry is powerful and effective in helping people—but mainly when used as a starting point. You see, many people are in need for a reason. In order be dependent on a system, we need to teach them to be dependent upon God. We need to develop a good mix of grace, mercy, wisdom, leading of the Spirit, and sound biblical principles, to release people into a personal walk with God.

When we minister with this mentality lives will be transformed into the image of Christ and people will begin to enjoy lives of abundance that will become a living testimony to those around them. They will no longer live as victims, but as sons of the Most High, walking in destiny and purpose.

STEWARDSHIP

A very important and clear principle that will help us understand everyone's responsibility is the principle of stewardship. Stewardship is not only applicable to finances, but to everything that God has entrusted us with. We are made stewards over whatever He has given us. A steward is the same as a manager. Everyone manages the things that God has given him. Stewardship will also give us insight into the responsibility that each person has in being stewards over the things that God has entrusted to them. Let's read about this in Matthew 25:14-30:

For the Kingdom of heaven is like a man traveling to a far country, who called his own servants and delivered his goods to them. And to one he gave five talents, to another two, and to another one, to each according to his own ability; and immediately he went on a journey. Then he who had received the five talents went and traded with them, and made another five talents. And likewise he who had received two gained two more also. But he who had received one went and dug in the ground, and hid his lord's money. After a long time the lord of those servants came and settled accounts with them. So he who had received five talents came and brought five other talents, saying, 'Lord, you delivered to me five talents; look, I have delivered to me two talents; look, I have gained two more talents besides them.' His lord said to him, 'Well done, good and faithful servant; you have been faithful over a few things, I will make you ruler over many things. Enter into the joy of your lord.' Then he who had received the one talent came and said, 'Lord, I knew you to be a hard man, reaping where you have not sown, and gathering where you have not scattered seed. And I was afraid, and went and hid

*your talent in the ground. Look, there you have what is yours.'
But his lord answered and said to him, 'You wicked and lazy
servant, you knew that I reap where I have not sown, and
gather where I have not scattered seed. So you ought to have
deposited my money with the bankers, and at my coming I
would have received back my own with interest. Therefore
take the talent from him, and give it to him who has ten talents. For to everyone who has, more will be given, and he will
have abundance; but from him who does not have, even what
he has will be taken away. And cast the unprofitable servant
into the outer darkness. There will be weeping and gnashing
of teeth.'*

In this story we notice several remarkable things. First, we can
conclude that God gives more to one person than to another.
Many times Christians have the socialistic mindset that we
need to share everything with everyone, but that is not biblical. And it doesn't matter how much He has given you. What
matters is that you are a faithful steward, because you will be
held accountable in the end. The fact that you are born with
little is not an excuse to not do anything.

Everyone has the God-given ability to take what they have
and to multiply it, regardless of how much they've been giv-
en. Not only do you have the ability, but it is expected that you
multiply. The kingdom of God is one of expansion, multiplication, and progression. Adam, who was made steward over the
Garden of Eden, was commissioned to multiply and expand
the kingdom over the face of the earth.

If we decide not to obey the instruction to use and multiply
the talents given to us by God, we find quite a shocking conse-
quence. Let's read verse 29 again:

*For to everyone who has, more will be given, and he will have
abundance; but from him who does not have, even what he
has will be taken away.*

It is quite clear that when you are not a good steward over the
things entrusted to you, God will take away what little you do

have and give it to him who already has. Some people are in need and suffer lack because God has taken away what little they did have.

It is within this context that I say that it is not righteous for us to always help those who are lacking. Sometimes the best help we can give is to teach the principles of stewardship.

Chapter Nine

THE GOSPEL OF THE KINGDOM

THE GOSPEL OF SALVATION

Apostolic reformation will impact the message the church has been preaching for year after year, by shifting it from a salvation-focused message to a kingdom-focused one. Growing up as a Christian, I was taught the "gospel of salvation" as being the ultimate and only real important part of the Christian message. Of course, the salvation message is where it all begins. In fact, without the message of the redeeming power of the blood of Jesus, there wouldn't be a church. Yet for years the church has limited herself by preaching a limited gospel. The preaching of salvation alone, without an understanding of taking dominion, will cause people to retreat from the frontlines and encourage them to become defensive. This escapist mentality must change.

For a long time, Christians have tried to change the world by preaching this defensive gospel. One of the main reasons why the church hasn't been successful in penetrating society is because of this limited message that tells people to be "saved from (fill in the blank)." This message communicates to the Christian community that they would be better off staying away from the very thing they were just saved from—which in turn causes the Church to become isolated from the rest of the world. When Jesus was on earth, He carried a message that went beyond simply being saved.

Whenever we look up the word "gospel" in the New Testament, we'll find that it's not only associated with salvation. Yes, salvation was a crucial part of the message that Jesus preached. But the words "gospel of salvation" are nowhere to be found in the Bible. Instead, Jesus uses the words "gospel of the kingdom." The word "kingdom" speaks about a greater dimension. In other words, the concept of the gospel of the kingdom contains the message of salvation but is not solely defined by it. The word "kingdom "speaks of government, authority, power, and dominion. The message that Jesus therefore we escape his authority by being saved. But the Word of God clearly says that we are not only called to be saved from this world but to rule over it by taking dominion.

WHAT WOULD JESUS DO?

For a modern-day illustration of this shift in the emphasis of our message, consider the popular W.W.J.D. (What Would Jesus Do?) question. The basic idea is very good. It teaches people to ask themselves the question "What Jesus Would Do?" in every situation they face. This is a key that will unlock a life of success. And yet, within a church that only preaches a gospel of salvation, the W.W.J.D. approach will only be partly effective. Whenever you ask people "What Would Jesus Do?" you'll likely discover that most people will try to find an answer to that question in the realm of the fruits of the Spirit.

The Church has taught people the humanistic message, that they can be effective in the world by being "different" in character. If we only behave joyful, kind, faithful and loving, people will surely notice Christ in us. Many people respond to W.W.J.D. through a behavioral decision which is based on the fruit of the Spirit. They think that walking in the fruit of the Spirit will help them penetrate society. They try to use the fruit of the Spirit as the spear point of their Christian walk. The truth is, I know some non-Christians who are much more kind and loving than many Christians I know!

As we study the life of Jesus and how He responded in difficult situations we can only conclude that we need to answer the W.W.J.D. question differently. Jesus didn't change the world by being kind, or nice to people. He wasn't necessarily always friendly, either. He changed the world by demonstrating the power of God. But when He saw a sick man, He healed him! When He saw someone who was possessed, He cast the devil out! He raised the dead! He calmed the storm! He put the ear back on the head of Malchus. What would Jesus do? He would demonstrate the kingdom! The anointing and power of God is the spear-point of the church, not character. The supernatural helps us penetrate society, instead of merely changing behavioral patterns. If we want to take true godly dominion, we will have to move in signs and wonders, and mighty deeds.

Does this mean that the fruit of the Spirit is not important? Of course not. The power of God is our spear-point, but the fruit of the Spirit is like the rod attached to the head of a spear. The head gives substance and weight to the spear, enabling it to penetrate the intended target.

A proper balance between the power of God and the fruit of the Spirit will cause the church to become effective and powerful. Both are needed. The answer to the W.W.J.D. question is found in both realms. The problem with the gospel of salvation is that it promotes only one realm, not the other. It will teach people to "be saved from," instead of teaching people to "rule over."

The reforming message of the apostolic church will teach people to take dominion, to be productive, to expand, and to advance the kingdom of God. This message goes beyond humanistic mindsets and an escapist mentality. When we preach the gospel of the kingdom of God we will manifest His glory throughout the whole earth.

ANOINTED TO PREACH THE GOSPEL

We are going to need the anointing of God to be able to preach a biblical gospel that will destroy the yokes of the enemy. The well-known scripture is found in Isaiah 61:1:

The Spirit of the Lord God is upon Me, Because the Lord has anointed Me to preach good tidings (to preach the gospel).

Isaiah 10:27 tells us:

And the yoke will be destroyed because of the anointing oil.

In other words, the only way we can effectively preach the gospel of Jesus Christ is by the anointing of God's Spirit. Let's take a look at Matthew 4:23:

And Jesus went about all Galilee, teaching in their synagogues, preaching the gospel of the Kingdom, and healing all kinds of sickness and all kinds of disease among the people. Then His fame went throughout all Syria; and they brought to Him all sick people who were afflicted with various diseases and torments, and those who were demon-possessed, epileptics, and paralytics; and He healed them. Great multitudes followed Him—from Galilee, and from Decapolis, Jerusalem, Judea, and beyond the Jordan.

Again we see that the message of Jesus wasn't limited to salvation. The reason the multitudes followed Him was because of His supernatural demonstration of the Holy Spirit and of power. The spear-point of His ministry was the supernatural. This is how He became"famous" in the whole region of Syria, not by being nice.

What is the other. Let's read John 3:3:

Jesus answered and said to him, 'Most assuredly, I say to you,unless one is born again, he cannot see the Kingdom of God.'

This scripture indicates that the condition for seeing the kingdom of God is rebirth, or in other words, salvation. Yet when we read on we see that there is another condition to entering the kingdom. We read about it in verse 5:

> Jesus answered, 'Most assuredly, I say to you, unless one is born of water and the Spirit, he cannot enter the Kingdom of God.'

In other words, there is a dimension in the kingdom of God that we can only experience once we are born of the Spirit. Once we have received the anointing of the Spirit we are not only able to see the kingdom but are also able to enter into it. Then, we will have access to all its resources. And because mankind can step from the natural realm into the spirit realm, we can enter the kingdom in the realm of the spirit, and take its blessings with us to the natural realm. The moment we take the riches of the kingdom of God with us to the natural realm, signs, wonders, and mighty deeds will follow.

We often pray, "Let your kingdom come; Your will be done on earth as it is in heaven!" But do we realize how this prayer will be answered? How does His kingdom become visible on earth? By building a great auditorium that will hold four thousand people? No. There are many ungodly buildings in the world that hold more than that! Will it be by promoting our events on advertising posters and TV spots? No.

This is not a unique concept for attracting people in the world, either. These things are not wrong, and many times God uses them, but they are not visual proof of His kingdom on earth. The only way we can see God's kingdom become visible in the earth is when we, His church, arise in authority and subdue darkness by the power and anointing of God's Spirit. Yet this will only happen when we enter the kingdom of God and take its riches with us into the natural realm. Luke 11:20 teaches us:

> But if I cast out demons with the finger of God, surely the Kingdom of God has come upon you.

Notice that Jesus teaches the same thing here. He declares

that once you see darkness subdued, then the kingdom of God has come. Salvation and anointing (baptism in the Holy Spirit) are both necessary ingredients for preaching and demonstrating the gospel.

Jesus also taught this principle to the apostles. Let's take a look at what it means to be filled with the Spirit of God.

BE FILLED WITH THE HOLY SPIRIT

Receiving the Holy Spirit" is described under the new covenant as two different experiences. The first is described in John 20:21-22, where we read about the appearance of Jesus just after His resurrection:

> So Jesus said to them again, 'Peace to you! As the Father has sent Me, I also send you.' And when He had said this, He breathed on them, and said to them, 'Receive the Holy Spirit.'

This specific event in the lives of the apostles caused them to be born again. From the moment Jesus declared these words they received salvation. In Romans 10:9 we read about the two conditions for salvation:

> ...that if you confess with your mouth the Lord Jesus and believe in your heart that God has raised Him from the dead, you will be saved.

Based on this verse we can conclude that the two requirements for salvation are confession with your mouth that Jesus is Lord and believing in your heart that God has raised Him from the dead.

Once someone meets these requirements, they will be saved. Jesus breathed on the apostles in John 20, which was the very moment they met both requirements of salvation for the first time in history. They believed in their hearts that He was risen. The result was salvation. The terminology Jesus used are the words "receive the Holy Spirit." We could call this experience of the receiving of the Holy Spirit the "Easter experience."

Now let's take a look at what happened after this. We read in the following scriptures that Jesus didn't want the apostles to immediately go and carry out their apostolic mandate.

In fact, He commanded them to go to Jerusalem first, so that they would have another Holy Spirit experience. Only after this experience did He send them. We read about Jesus' words concerning this second Holy Spirit experience in Acts 1:4.

And being assembled together with them, He commanded them not to depart from Jerusalem, but to wait for the Promise of the Father, 'which,' He said, 'you have heard from Me; for John truly baptized with water, but you shall be baptized with the Holy Spirit not many days from now.'

Jesus says this after giving the apostles their commission in Mark 16:15 to go into the whole world to preach the gospel. This sounds strange. But chronologically this is what happens. Jesus gives the disciples the Holy Spirit after breathing on them after his resurrection. He commissions them to go into the whole world and preach the gospel. Then He immediately tells them not to go yet, but to wait in Jerusalem where they will receive the Holy Spirit. But did or did they not already receive the Holy Spirit? Yes and no! Yes, they were saved and therefore received the indwelling of the Spirit of God.

Yet in order to carry out the apostolic mandate, another Holy Spirit experience of a different dimension was needed, which we could call the "Pentecostal experience." We read about this second experience in Acts 2:4:

And they were all filled with the Holy Spirit and began to speak with other tongues, as the Spirit gave them utterance.

Again they were filled with the Holy Spirit, but this time the result was not salvation. As we read earlier, they had already received that. This time the result of receiving the Holy Spirit was receiving the power to do. Acts 1:8 gives them an explanation for why they had to wait:

But you shall receive power when the Holy Spirit has come upon you; and you shall be witnesses to Me in Jerusalem, and in all Judea and Samaria, and to the end of the earth.

Salvation wasn't enough to bring the gospel to the four corners of the earth. They needed another dimension added to them, which would give them the power to carry out the apostolic mandate.

Many churches today go to the ends of the earth without having both of the Holy Spirit experiences. They try to do what Jesus would do without the power of the Spirit. They preach the gospel of salvation, which is only effective to a certain extent. However, the apostolic church realizes that without the power and anointing of the Spirit it is impossible to go into the whole world and fulfill its mandate.

The apostolic church is called to carry a message that doesn't end with salvation, but that only begins with salvation. Those within this move of God will preach and demonstrate the gospel of the kingdom of God with unlimited power, causing nations to be changed by the outpouring of the Holy Spirit.

Chapter Ten

A ROYAL PRIESTHOOD, A HOLY NATION

ORGANIZATION OR ORGANISM

While observing the spiritual climate of the church, I have come to believe that another transition needs to take place. The established church, which is kept together mainly by institutional rules, regulations and business principles, needs to be redefined by covenant relationships and lineage. Not that organizational activity and performance is all bad, but rather it needs to be backed up by godly relationships that will distinguish the body of Christ from those in the world. God has called the church to be a holy nation, not a successful company. Therefore we need to profile ourselves as a nation that is kept together by father-son relationships, not by work contracts and hire-fire mentalities. The church that is willing to work with these principles will display an accurate image of God in the earth, causing our communities to be changed by the power of the Holy Spirit.

Apostolic reformation will release a needed awareness which will cause us to go from a static, institutional structure, to a dynamic, tribal structure. Apostolic reformation will help us understand that we are an organism, not an organization. It's clear, especially in the Western world, that the church is often no different from a worldly organization run by business principles. A big auditorium, a pastor on the payroll, a tax exempt number and the two hours between 10 a.m. And noon on Sunday are often the elements that define churches all around the world. Of themselves, these elements are neutral and God can and will use them to minister to His people. Yet as much as business principles need to be applied to reach a level of excellence and professionalism, they are only tools given to help the church, not what defines her.

The culture among church leaders is often unhealthy because they base their ministerial decisions on promotional possibilities, instead of on their divine call and destiny. Pastors are leaving congregations whenever another opportunity arises that better suits their planned career path. Spiritual leadership is then hired once the majority decides, and as long as a business agreement is signed.

Spiritual leaders can also be fired this same way, if he or she becomes too confronting. This democratic voice and lack of commitment works both ways.

Many congregations consist of "churchgoers" as opposed to a people who are the church. Many church memberships are based on satisfactory consumption of the church event agenda; once people are no longer satisfied with the activities offered, they will leave and find a "better" church.

The apostolic church will be completely different. It will root out man-pleasing mentalities and mindsets and establish a healthy, God-fearing culture that will nurture and develop long-term covenant relationships.

A HOLY NATION

So if the church is not supposed to be an organization or business, what should the culture and structure of the apostolic church look like?

This question is answered in Exodus 19:6, where we read the following:

And you shall be to Me a Kingdom of priests and a holy nation.

These are the Words of God concerning His covenant with the people of Israel. In fact, this is the same promise that God gave Abraham years before in Genesis 12:2:

I will make you a great nation; I will bless you And make your name great; And you shall be a blessing.

In both portions of scripture, God promises to make His people both a kingdom and a nation. Therefore, whoever believes in Christ is called to be part of this great nation. We are all the offspring of Abraham.

We are all part of a people that came forth from the seed of Abraham.

We are all from his lineage. We are a kingdom of priests. We are a holy nation. Theologically, most of us embrace this concept. Yet we do not see this "nation principle" manifested in everyday church life. This is where, again, we discover the importance of this current apostolic move. This reformation will bring us a clear understanding of this concept, causing the church to be completely transformed.

A NATION DEFINED

So what makes a nation a nation? The answer is quite simple. A nation, or a people, is born out of one person. The children of Israel were considered a nation because they were the seed of Abraham. They were his offspring. They had the same blood running through their veins. They were the same race, with a similar genetic structure. And so we see how God always works through lineage or family lines. He always works trans-generationally. He is not only the God of Abraham, but the God of Abraham, Isaac, and Jacob.

Naturally speaking, whenever someone is born, they are always born as part of a people. Everyone is born into a lineage and is part of a nation. When you are born Dutch, you will stay Dutch forever. However, it is not your passport that defines the nation you are part of, but rather the blood that you received from your father. You may even live in another country, or possess a different passport, but nothing will change the blood that flows through your veins. A nation is a nation because of the fact that everyone is kept together by a family relational network. No one can ever change this. In the same way, the structure of the church is formed with fathers, mothers, brothers, sisters, uncles, aunts, grandfathers, grandmothers, and so on. These are the types of relationships that should define the church. This is the structure that God designed for His people.

Why is it so important to realize that we are part of a nation, and not an organization? Does it make that big of a difference? Yes, because once we realize that we are part of an organic family structure, we will start to discover who we are. And once we discover who we are, we'll refuse to think with the old mentality that sees fellow believers as colleagues, bosses, managers, and employees. Throughout the Word of God we discover that whenever a name is mentioned, the name of the person's father is mentioned as well.

Why is that? Because the identity of a person is found in the father. That's why the Bible doesn't just speak about David, but also about David, the son of Jesse. The "son of Jesse" part is added to his name to define the identity of David. By doing that people knew who they were talking about. It not only gave the son identity but also authority and recognition. Therefore we see that identity received through lineage was very important and powerful in the historical period of the Bible.

This is why there are endless genealogies mentioned throughout the Bible. It is obvious to note how God works though the generations. His plan gets worked out through fathers, through sons, through grandchildren, and on until the restoration of all things will usher in the second coming of

Christ. Who are you? Are you a son, or are you a hireling? Only when we think and live with a lineage mindset can we truly be a son.

Chapter Eleven

FOUR LEVELS OF IDENTITY

· ·

The biblical structure of the nation of Israel gives us a clear blueprint for the structure of the church of Jesus.

As we read about God's people in the Old Testament we discover four levels of identity in each individual. It is very important to recognize all four of these levels in our own lives if we want to be effective and productive in walking out our destinies. An Old Testament believer could be identified on four levels:

- He was part of the nation Israel
- He was part of a tribe
- He was part of a family
- He had his own characteristics and features that made him unique

For the New Testament believer there are similar levels of identity from which we can define our lives. Everyone who desires to grow to a mature Christian will enter a process which will bring them through these four stages. In this process we will discover who we really are and what we are supposed to do.

THE IDENTITY OF A SON OF GOD

It is very important for every believer to be confident in their identity as a son of God. After all, once we are born again, we can call God our Father. We read about this in John 1:12-13:

> *But as many as received Him, to them He gave the right to become children of God, to those who believe in His name: who were born, not of blood, nor of the will of the flesh, nor of the will of man, but of God.*

The most important thing is that we know that we are children of God. We need to have an experience with God through which we will receive the revelation that we are His beloved sons. Even Jesus had such an experience. It is important to note that He had this experience before He began His ministry. We can read about it in Matthew 3:16-17:

> *When He had been baptized, Jesus came up immediately from the water; and behold, the heavens were opened to Him, and He saw the Spirit of God descending like a dove and alighting upon Him. And suddenly a voice came from heaven, saying, 'This is My beloved Son, in whom I am well pleased.'*

When we are baptized and begin our walk as a Christian, we need to have a similar experience. Before we do anything in ministry we need a personal revelation of who we are in Christ. We must be confident in the fact that we are sons of the Most High. We need to know that He loves us and that He is pleased with us. This is the first and most important level of identity, as becoming a son of God separates us from the world and makes us part of His kingdom of priests.

TRIBAL IDENTITY

Even though it is true that being a son of God is one of the most important steps in our Christian walk, it doesn't mean that's all there is. If that were the case, then we would all be the same and there would be no diversity within the church. It is important for everyone to discover who they are, or in other words what their individual identity is. Once we discover that we will know how we fit in the whole picture.

As we look at the Old Testament structure of Israel, we discover that this nation was divided into twelve different tribes. It is important to realize that this tribal division of the people of God is contrary to the denominational division of the church as we have known it. Each person of a particular tribe could be traced back through their genealogy to the same person, the tribal father. In fact, all those born of a certain tribe are, in a sense, part of the same lineage or family. In the same way, when someone is born again he not only receives his identity as son of God, but will also receive a specific, tribal identity that will define this person's purpose and call in the earth. So what then distinguishes one tribe from another? In Genesis 49:1-2 we read:

And Jacob called his sons and said, 'Gather together, that I may tell you what shall befall you in the last days: Gather together and hear, you sons of Jacob, And listen to Israel your father.'

This portion of scripture teaches us about the origin of the tribal structure of Israel. Jacob called all his sons together before his death, to share with them their purpose and the purpose of their lineage. He took the time to prophesy identity, destiny and life into his sons. These words, spoken by their father, gave Jacob's twelve sons direction for the future and a specific purpose that would distinguish them from the others. Each lineage received their own assignment and function, and eventually even their own inheritance in the land of promise. For example, the tribe of Levi served in the house of the Lord, while the lineage of Judah was called for frontline warfare. The Levites received the tithe of the people as their inheritance, while the other tribes each received a specific part of the Promised Land as their inheritance.

Under the new covenant we can see the same tribal identity

principles at work. God the Father has called together some of His sons to speak identity and purpose into their lives. These divine words will divide the church into different tribal identities, propelling each lineage into its own unique, God-given direction. This, in turn, will cause those mature sons to be tribal heads or patriarchs over an entire lineage of sons with a similarity of purpose in the earth. It is then the task of these patriarchs to release the younger generations into the mandate and purpose that God has given them through Him. Why? Because the very structure of the apostolic church is founded upon this tribal principle. A patriarch or a tribal father is not chosen by men but is hand-selected and ordained by God Himself. It was in this same way that God chose Noah, Abraham, Moses, and many others. The key is that He chooses those who are willing to become tribal fathers within the new covenant. For even as Jesus Himself selected His twelve disciples, so God alone will determine the patriarchs of the New Testament tribes.

God has destined each and every one of us to fit into one of the tribal identities given to the church. Each Christian is born again with a specific purpose and destiny, and is called to be part of a specific lineage of people. Biologically, there are always two elements that we directly inherit from our natural father; our blood and our bone structure. Our blood and bones define who we are. Therefore we can conclude that identity is received directly from the father. In the same way the tribal father passes on the bone structure and bloodline, which is the very identity of the tribe. In the same way we can only be part of one bloodline in the natural, spiritually we can only be part of one tribal identity.

In a certain way every person in a tribe will look the same. Why is that? Because they have the same father! They have the same bones and they have the same blood. Their inner configuration is the same. Because of this same identity, each New Testament tribe will have a specific corporate identity. God works through relationships, lineage, and covenant, while the majority of the church thinks in terms of institutions or organizations.

But remember that a spiritual father raises sons, not employees. It is a tribe, not an organization that is birthed when God breathes upon man. Whether or not he receives a high income, he will stay the father of the tribe. There is nothing that can take away fatherhood. Once you have a son, you will always have a son, whether you like it or not. It is not a temporary position you can fill but rather a responsibility that rests upon your shoulders. Once we begin to realize this we'll no longer perceive spiritual leaders as controlling, autocratic people. More than anything we'll begin to see them as loving fathers who want the best for us.

Once we transition to a tribal mentality, we will no longer hop from one church to another, because we'll understand that we are part of a lineage and that our lineage won't change by simply becoming a member somewhere else. When you have identified your spiritual father, you will no longer desire to continually change churches, or to attend a church based on your opinion of their leadership. Once a son, always a son! Though this is true, we should never use this as an argument or as a tool to control and keep people from making their own choices. People are always free to go where they want—even sons! In Luke 15:11-13 we read the following:

> Then He said: 'A certain man had two sons. And the younger of them said to his father, "Father, give me the portion of goods that falls to me." So he divided to them his livelihood. And not many days after, the younger son gathered all together, journeyed to a far country, and there wasted his possessions with prodigal living.'

A son will always have the father's permission to leave the house, as a true spiritual father never controls or manipulates his son into staying in a place he does not want to be. In Luke 15 the youngest son wanted to leave his father's house. Instead of forcing him to stay, the father released him, even giving him his inheritance.

This principle should also be applied within the church. There should be room, within a godly structure, for a son to leave. Yet note that, although he left his father's house and squandered his inheritance, the young man remained a son. Being a son never changes. Once a son, always a son.

But although a father's house holds many blessing, that doesn't mean life will always be easy. The father disciplines, corrects, and tells us the truth. This is the function of a father, and because of these dynamics it sometimes seems easier to leave your father's house and become a hireling somewhere else. After all, an employer is only interested in whether or not you are finishing your work. At the end of the day you will get your reward based upon the work that you have done, by means of a paycheck. In some ways, working within a business relationship like this might be easier.

A father won't give wages. A father may even give his son something he (the son) didn't work for. A father is not only interested in the work you do but also in you. And a father will give you an inheritance that goes far beyond mere wages. Your inheritance is one of the main reasons you need to identify your spiritual father. If you do not function under a spiritual father who is operating within a godly lineage, then there will be no inheritance. An inheritance comes from your father. For example, when the people of Israel identified their spiritual (tribal) father, they received a specific piece of land as an inheritance.

Just imagine for a minute that an Old Testament Israelite didn't know which tribe he was from. Where would he live? Where would he belong? How would he live? In the Old Testament it was impossible to get a piece of land for your family if you didn't know your lineage. If this was the case, the only option for survival would be to become someone's slave and receive limited wages. However, God doesn't want to limit us. His desire is for us to be His heirs and co-heirs with Christ. And yet it is only through identifying our predestined lineage that we will be fully able to receive our divine inheritance.

We read an interesting story in Ezra 2:59:

And these were the ones who came up from Tel Melah, Tel Harsha, Cherub, Addan, and Immer; but they could not identify their father's house or their genealogy, whether they were of Israel.

This scripture talks about a certain people that wanted to join Israel in rebuilding the walls of Jerusalem. We read that "they could not identify their father's house." In other words, they didn't know where they fit in. They were wandering. Their identity was not clear because they didn't know their genealogy. As we read further we see the following in verse 62:

These sought their listing among those who were registered by genealogy, but they were not found; therefore they were excluded from the priesthood as defiled.

Because their lineage was unclear, they were excluded from the priesthood. They could only be used in a limited way. The same principle is true for us when we are unable to identify our father's house. We will be limited in our ministry. We will be excluded from different dimensions of ministry that are only available for sons in the house. A son is authorized to work within the inheritance of the father. By working with his received inheritance a son is not limited by his individual ability to produce, but is well able to go far beyond his own potential. The inheritance of the father, combined with the personal potential of the son, will cause his success to multiply exceedingly.

FAMILY IDENTITY

The "local church" in the old school of thought is an independent unit that often limits itself to one building and one city. That specific local church grows when there are more people in that specific building in that city on a Sunday morning. Many times church growth is measured by these parameters alone. Church growth in light of a true apostolic church and within a tribal mentality, however, will think outside the box of a local church. Someone's tribal identity is not necessarily linked to their geographic location. You can go anywhere in the world, but that will not change your blood or your bone structure. The apostolic anointing sends sons into the world to different locations. These sons will reproduce and become fathers themselves. Under the old mindset, when someone leaves a church to go to live in a new location, it would mean that the church would become smaller. This is not so within the apostolic mindset.

The apostolic community would see this as tribal growth, rather than local decrease. As a matter a fact, this is the only way that a tribe can become a tribe. It is only when the patriarch raises up sons and sends them out to reproduce, to become fathers of their own children, that his tribal fatherhood will be established.

It is absolutely necessary for a father to raise and release his sons into their own destiny. Yes, a father disciplines, corrects, and even controls sometimes in a healthy way. He gives assignments, chores around the house, and instructions for our future. And even though we recognize the high value of these things, we should come to the point where we are no longer leaning on the instruction of our father only. In other words, we need to come to a place of maturity where we are able to make our own decisions. The spiritual father doesn't want us to take on a slave mentality for the rest of our lives. His desire is to raise us up to maturity. He does so by using discipline and instruction as a means of bringing us to a place we'll call manhood.

It's important to recognize that the tools a father uses in raising up sons are not a goal in and of themselves. For example, a father's discipline will lead his sons to a place where they are well able to make their own decisions with assurance and accuracy. However, many spiritual leaders and even those who function as fathers, fail to understand this dynamic and its importance within sonship. They teach and apply the principles of discipline and fatherhood in order to keep the sons under their control, no matter their spiritual age. They do not recognize that as their sons mature, the dynamics of these principles change. In Genesis 2:24 we read about this profound principle:

Therefore a man shall leave his father and mother and be joined to his wife, and they shall become one flesh.

This scripture describes the godly principle of fatherhood. This is what it is all about, yet many do not understand it. Of course this verse speaks about natural fatherhood, but we can apply it spiritually as well. It is the assignment of the father to bring his sons to maturity through discipline and instruction. A real father understands that discipline leads to freedom, not bondage. He also understands that in each of his son's lives there comes a point where he will "leave" his father. This is not a negative decision in which the son rejects the father, but rather a change in the type of relationship between the father and son.

Naturally speaking, when a child is only twelve years old you may tell him to help with the groceries, pull the weeds, and take out the garbage. When he disobeys, you will discipline him. Yet, as your son matures, he will come to a point where he will need to stand on his own two feet. He will leave his father, get married, and begin his own family. This is not an act of rebellion, nor the result of unhealthy independence, but rather the healthy maturing of a son who is now grown. If the father has completed his assignment well, the son will know and respect the heart of his father. Because of this, they will still be strongly connected—not only by blood, but also by their relationship which has developed throughout the years. The only thing that changes when a son "leaves" his father is that the relationship goes from discipline and instruction to counsel and advice.

When someone fails to recognize these dynamics there is the danger of having a wrong order in the church. When a season of discipline doesn't gradually mature into a season of counsel and advice, the discipline which was good yesterday will become unhealthy control and manipulation today. When a son is established in the identity of his father and leaves, he is now ready to reproduce and become a father himself. He is now ready to make his own decisions. He has the structure and the bones of his father, but he will give birth to his own family. He will do things differently. Maybe he will drive another kind of car, or live in a totally different sort of house. Yet deep within him the identity of the father has been established.

This apostolic lineage will also have its influence within the context of the local church. Contrary to the old order local church mentality, the apostolic church will be focused on sending people out, and stimulating people to have their own family expression. A tribal apostolic church is therefore one church in a multiplicity of locations and expressions. A true spiritual father will always encourage his sons to go and reproduce themselves. He will send them to become fathers in their own right, which in turn causes him to become a grandfather.

By this principle new "local churches" will be established in an organic way. New family expressions within one apostolic tribe will begin coming forth.

INDIVIDUAL IDENTITY

In teaching tribal identity principles there is always the danger that people will start to believe that we all need to be the same. People may think that tribal identity means that we need to look the same, act the same, and minister the same way. Yet the contrary is true.

When we talk about identity we are not talking about a worldly identity rooted in natural things such as fashion, hype, and cultural behavior, but about a spiritual identity. It is about the spiritual substance that a tribe carries. The inner configuration of the spirit is what has the same structure. You produce the same sound. Yet again, it is not a natural sound or style, but a sound in the Spirit. You operate within the same frequency. You are focused the same way and carry the same message. You are one in spirit, but not necessarily one in outward behavior. Of course sons take after their father, that's the same both naturally and spiritually. Yet individual characteristics need to be recognized, allowed, and even encouraged in order to establish each individual within the tribal ministry. Yes, I've got my father's blood and yes, I've got my father's bones, but there are still things that are unique about me. We need to remember that God creates every individual with unique characteristics and qualities in order to display His manifold grace through mankind.

Another important thing to remember is this: the measure in which God can work through an individual depends on the level in which this individual can be himself. In other words, if we are continually trying to be someone we are not, we limit the flow of God's Spirit through our lives. We are who we are in our own unique way. Everyone was created with his or her own unique style. One preacher's expression might be dynamic and loud while another's is calm and slow. Both expressions can work; it all depends on the individual's identity. When a calm teacher tries to be like the loud, dynamic preacher, people will sense that he is not himself and therefore will not receive his message. The opposite is also true. When a wild preacher tries to be all quiet and calm, people will look at him as if he's crazy. People sense when you are fake. People will notice if you are not yourself. For this reason it is very important that we minister within our own personal identity. Be yourself within the framework of the apostolic identity of your tribe and you will be powerful and fruitful.

Chapter Twelve

THE POWER OF UNITY

. . . .

MULTIPLICATION OF AUTHORITY

One of the characteristics of apostolic reformation is the way it looks at unity in relationship to other churches. Tremendous power is released when churches operate in unity. When God's people are one in spirit the powers of hell tremble and rulers of the air will bow down. This principle is mentioned in the Bible in Leviticus 26:8:

And five of you shall chase an hundred, and a hundred of you shall put ten thousand to flight: and your enemies shall fall before you by the sword.

There is a multiplication of authority in unity. Unity is a crucial element on our road to success. I have met many fellow believers who have put a lot of time and energy into fostering unity among different denominations within a region, yet none of their efforts have seen much fruit.

The reason for this is their efforts were rooted in a wrong perception of unity. Only people with an apostolic mindset are able to walk in true, biblical unity. This is the kind of unity that has eternal value.

When a church lacks the apostolic dimension, efforts in the name of unity will ultimately fail. The short-term result may appear to be some measure of unity between various churches, but unless the apostolic anointing is involved it will not last. Ephesians 4:11-16:

And he gave some, apostles; and some, prophets; and some, evangelists; and some, pastors and teachers; For the perfecting of the saints, for the work of the ministry, for the edifying of the body of Christ: Till we all come in the unity of the faith, and of the knowledge of the Son of God, unto a perfect man, unto the measure of the stature of the fullness of Christ: That we henceforth be no more children, tossed to and fro, and carried about with every wind of doctrine, by the sleight of men, and cunning craftiness, whereby they lie in wait to deceive; But speaking the truth in love, may grow up into him in all things, which is the head, even Christ: From whom the whole body fitly joined together and compacted by that which every joint supplieth, according to the effectual working in the measure of every part, maketh increase of the body unto the edifying of itself in love.

These bold words speak about "the unity of the faith" within the body of Christ as a whole. They also give us both the vision for and the strategy on how to reach this unity. It is clear that unity is only established within the context of active fivefold ministry. The complete spectrum of active fivefold ministry causes unity to become a reality. Because the perfecting of the saints can only take place when we are exposed to all five of these equipping dimensions, the unity of the faith can only be established once the apostolic anointing is involved. And so we see how the office of the apostle plays a crucial role in the joining together of the body of Christ.

On God's prophetic timetable we are now at a time in which the office of the apostle is being restored to the church. Only when this has fully taken place will the fivefold wineskin be complete, resulting in true biblical unity.

DENOMINATIONAL UNITY

We read in Ephesians 3:10:

To the intent that now unto the principalities and powers in heavenly places might be known by the Church the manifold wisdom of God, According to the eternal purpose which he purposed in Christ Jesus our Lord: In whom we have boldness and access with confidence by the faith of him. Wherefore I desire that ye faint not at my tribulations for you, which is your glory.

This verse about the manifold wisdom of God is a very popular one used by Christians to promote unity among different churches and denominations. Their philosophy is that every denomination on the earth represents a different flavor or color. In combining these colors or flavors, the manifold wisdom of God will then be revealed.

However, the starting point of this view is distorted and inaccurate, as it suggests that each denomination carries a portion of the manifold wisdom of God. The assumption that each individual denomination represents a specific color or identity is wrong.

Denominations are never rooted in identity or color, but always in doctrinal belief and in the way they interpret the Bible. Color speaks about expression and identity, while denominations are rooted in truths that were established in a past move of God. Contrary to doctrine, expression or identity cannot be labeled as good or bad. What makes a Baptist a Baptist? Answer: his doctrinal belief. What makes a Catholic a Catholic? Answer: the fact that he believes in a certain way of interpreting the Bible that is dictated by the Catholic Church. What makes a charismatic Christian charismatic? Answer: the fact that his doctrine tells him that the charisma gifts of the Holy Spirit are given to him today. Every denomination has its own doctrinal beliefs. There are major differences in the doctrinal convictions of the different denominations. Their denominational existence is rooted in these differences. Clearly, then, denominational unity has nothing to do with the manifold wisdom of God, because He happens to only have one doctrine! It is impossible to have two opposite doctrines and believe that both are an expression of God. The idea that when these two opposite doctrines are somehow combined, then God's manifold wisdom is being displayed, is foolishness.

Doctrinal differences make it difficult to establish strong, long-term unity among different denominations. Even though denominational unity may be a noble purpose, I dare to state that it is an impossible. A denomination has become a denomination because it has decided to no longer stay in line with the present-truth revelation of God's Spirit. When you place a denomination and its origin on a historic time-line, you will discover that, at some point, this particular group of people refused to stay in line with the fresh revelation of the Spirit of God of that day. A church split is inevitable. Those who desire to move on do not necessarily want to create division, but there is no way for them to remain a part of their denomination and still advance and emerge in the earth while there are others who do not want to move on. Many times "small" groups of Christians that split off the established church are looked at as people who don't value unity. Yet the truth is that the stubbornness of the established religious order of the day is what caused the division.

Observing these dynamics in church history, we have to wonder if it is realistic to think that denominations that are even more established in their doctrine now will suddenly change their mind and decide to partake in a present-truth move of God. I am not saying it is impossible. I realize that there have been recent moves of God in which different denominations were involved. The revival in Argentina, for example, was triggered by a coalition of different denominations. Yet if we study this revival in more detail, we find that all the denominations involved came to the point where they didn't care about their doctrinal rules and regulations anymore. All they wanted was a move of God. Both Baptist and Pentecostal were speaking in tongues. There were no more major doctrinal disputes. Even though they were labeled denominational, their background was unimportant: God moved, and that was all they cared about. The Baptist still called himself Baptist, but the denominational doctrine of the Baptist denomination was no longer of importance. All denominations involved in this move believed in the same foundational things, and were in line with the present-day revelation of God. They shifted from their denominational paradigm to an accurate view of what God was doing in their day. Maybe there were minor differences, but they were willing to change their doctrinal belief and come into one accord. This allowed them to cast out demons, heal the sick, and initiate a move of God in the earth.

In other words, the unity that played a crucial part in the Argentina revival was not a denominational unity, but a true unity of faith. They became of like faith. Their focus was on the move of God rather than on their doctrine. Purposely trying to bring together different denominations in order to make them one will never work. I believe unity is essential to the body of Christ, yet I think it is unwise to put a lot of time, energy, and money into bringing together different denominations just for the sake of unity. Never make unity your goal, but make the move of God your goal. Get your focus right. Once we do that, unity will simply be a result.

HORIZONTAL OR VERTICAL UNITY

One of the most popular scriptures to promote unity is found in John 17:20-21:

> *I do not pray for these alone, but also for those who will believe in Me through their word; that they all may be one, as You, Father, are in Me, and I in You; that they also may be one in Us, that the world may believe that You sent Me.*

Many believers apply these verses only horizontally, believing that Jesus is emphasizing the need for them to be one with each other Yet when we look at this verse a little more closely, we discover another interpretation. Jesus doesn't pray that the believers may be one with each other horizontally; He prays a vertical prayer. He prays that they (the believers) may be one with the Father in the same way He was one with the Father. He prays for a unity with the Father, not for a unity among each other. His focus is on how the believers should relate to the Father (vertically), not how the believers should relate to each other (horizontally). When we try to focus on horizontal unity there is the danger that we might feel the need to leave our unity with the Father in order to accomplish unity with each other. If we want to become one with all Christians, there is the danger of compromising present-truth revelation. Yet when a vertical unity with the Father is established, we will automatically be one with fellow believers who have that same unity with the Father. Once we see this, we recognize that true unity is a result of being one with the Father, rather than a goal in itself. As we are open, we automatically meet fellow believers "in the Father," no matter their denominational background. "In the Father" is an atmosphere that joins together everyone found in that place.

When our focus is unity with the Father, religious institutions will be filtered out automatically. Remember Babylon and Egypt: we want to avoid putting lots of energy into people who refuse to leave those places. In Ezra 3:1 we read: "And when the seventh month was come, and the children of Israel were in the cities, the people gathered themselves together as one man to Jerusalem." The rebuilding of the walls of Jerusalem was accomplished in the spirit of unity. Yet the only people who were able to help were those who had gone to the geographical location of Jerusalem. We can only work in unity with those who have accurately positioned themselves in the spirit. Only those who have migrated to a place of destiny can be part of the team. Those enslaved in Babylon and Egypt are disqualified.

The apostolic church doesn't strive for unity. All she does is position herself to be one with the Father, with an open heart. Then God begins connecting her to those who do the same. Suddenly, as those who are in unity with the Father, we may meet someone and our spirit jumps on the inside, as God is connecting groups and individuals with like faith. This doesn't mean that we need to close ourselves and reject other denominations. As a matter a fact, we should be open to everyone, and preach the message God has given us, which is a message of freedom. But we shouldn't put time and energy into religious activity that is doomed to fail.

We need to preach reformation to everyone around us, pulling people from the religious order like pulling David out of Saul's house, by bringing them in line with the present-truth message of God. Many denominational people long for a life-giving apostolic message. The problem is often with the "pharaohs," or leaders; they will not let them go. The people first need to leave their place of bondage in order to become usable before God. Don't try to change Pharaoh, but leave him at once. We don't go into Egypt to become one with those in bondage, but pray that those in bondage will leave Egypt and become one with us.

THE MANIFOLD WISDOM OF GOD DISPLAYED

One of the core responsibilities of an apostle is to establish sound doctrine. Once the fivefold ministry operates as one unit (Eph. 4:11), we notice in Ephesians 4:14-15 how an accurate doctrine is then established:

...that we should no longer be children, tossed to and fro and carried about with every wind of doctrine, by the trickery of men, in the cunning craftiness of deceitful plotting, but, speaking the truth in love, may grow up in all things into Him who is the head, Christ.

As God's people submit to apostolic reformation, the fivefold ministry gifts will be able to establish sound doctrine within the people. The office of the apostle completes the full spectrum of the fivefold ministry, enabling the saints to accurately teach the word of God. One of the problems with many of the denominational churches of the day is that they primarily operate without the apostolic dimension. We, as the body of Christ, need to recognize the dynamics of this current reformation so that the false winds of doctrine and denominational convictions and opinions of man can be dismantled.

Only then will there be a change in the structure of the church. It was never meant to be denominational, but rather tribal. The tribes of the Old Testament were not different because of their doctrinal belief, but rather because of their identity, purpose, and destiny. They all believed the same thing, yet they were different by the call of God. When there are no doctrinal stumbling blocks it is very easy to become one. It is in this place that we are all one in the Father, but we also recognize a different call and destiny. Every tribe knows who they are and where they are going. And although we recognize differences in the other tribes, we realize that we are connected to them by spirit. It is only through the Father that the different tribes will be joined together as one people, the people of God.

A SCEPTER RISES UP

A mature, apostolic people understand their place and purpose within the body of Christ in the same way the Old Testament tribes knew their place. They understand their purpose and destiny in the earth. They are aware of where they are from, and where they are going. This secure identity results in a strong focus on the purposes of God for the tribe. This kind of specific focus and vision is often something that is lacking in the denominational church. The vision and focus of the established order is often limited to a general vision such as "reaching people," or "loving each other."

In the old school of thought, projects and activities were some of the main methods used in an attempt to create unity. The thought was that in doing things together and by working out the same vision, unity had to come. These kind of citywide initiatives provided vision for those groups without a clear focus. But for a tribal, apostolic church these initiatives are many times a distraction from their true purpose. Yes, we all have the same mission: world harvest! But by no means should we all work out the same vision. When we read the book of Ezra, we can clearly see that every group of people had their own focus and their own part of the wall to build. Therefore everyone had to position himself in such a way that he could complete his part of the wall. Of course you first need to find out what your assignment is before you begin building, but then you have to stick to your assignment and your assignment alone. No one else is going to complete your task—it is yours to complete. Therefore, by launching citywide activities, there is a danger that people will leave their part of the wall to work together in "unity" on something they weren't meant to be doing. We should never leave our God-given vision in order to work within someone else's.

Tribal unity is the only type of unity that will have a long-term effect. It is not something that can be created by initiating a corporate activity, nor by compromising doctrine. It is something that can be done by spirit alone. Each tribe is different in its purpose and vision.

Each tribe knows its place within the camp. Each tribe has its own assignment from God and, although each one is different, we are one people baptized into one body. True unity will be the result of each individual tribe positioning itself according to God's plan. It is in this way that we will truly work together as one people, completing a singular mission by doing different things. In the Old Testament we see a clear picture of the tribal positioning of the people of Israel in Numbers 24:2:

And Balaam raised his eyes, and saw Israel encamped according to their tribes; and the Spirit of God came upon him.

When the prophet Balaam saw the accurate tribal positioning of God's people, the Spirit of God was released and he began to prophesy. In verse 17-19 he declares:

I see Him, but not now; I behold Him, but not near; A Star shall come out of Jacob; A Scepter shall rise out of Israel, And batter the brow of Moab, And destroy all the sons of tumult. And Edom shall be a possession; Seir also, his enemies, shall be a possession, While Israel does valiantly. Out of Jacob One shall have dominion, And destroy the remains of the city.

As Balaam saw tribal order and unity, he received a revelation by spirit of the scepter that would rise out of Israel. A scepter is symbolic of authority and government. Balaam also began to declare that "he that shall have dominion shall come forth." This is what true unity does; it releases power and authority. As the tribal apostolic church begins to position herself accurately and according to God's purposes, she will receive the "scepter" to rule and reign on the earth.

This principle is confirmed by the account of King David found in 1 Samuel 5:1-3:

Then all the tribes of Israel came to David at Hebron and spoke, saying, 'Indeed we are your bone and your flesh. Also, in time past, when Saul was king over us, you were the one who led Israel out and brought them in; and the LORD said to you, 'You shall shepherd My people Israel, and be ruler over Israel.' Therefore all the elders of Israel came to the king at Hebron, and King David made a covenant with them at Hebron before the LORD. And they anointed David king over Israel.

David represented the new order of the day. He was destined by God to become the king of Israel. The mandate to rule over Israel was upon his shoulders. He represented the current move of God of those days. Yet it wasn't until all twelve tribes came to David in agreement and unity, and acknowledged him as king, that the kingly anointing was restored in Israel. This kingly anointing then enabled David to conquer the city of Zion. It was the city of God, the place where God's throne was established, the city of divine government.

And so we see that denominational unity without unity in the spirit causes confusion, frustration, and compromise, but tribal unity through the spirit releases the authority to establish divine government in the earth.

Chapter Thirteen

DESTROYING OUR TEMPLE MENTALITY

THE UTTERMOST PARTS OF THE EARTH

As we have seen in previous chapters, an actual reformation is never a goal in itself. It simply prepares the way by renewing our minds so that we are able to transition into the new order of God. Reformation always points to "He who comes after me." It prepares the way for the coming of the new move of God. This current reformation will lead us into the full manifestation of the apostolic move. This move will then cause us to establish the kingdom of God in the four corners of the earth. A transition from revelation and reformation in the church to the manifestation of God's kingdom in the nations of the world needs to take place. We need to recognize this time of transition, otherwise we will stagnate.

Let's read again the apostolic words Jesus declared to his apostles in Acts 1:8:

> *But you shall receive power when the Holy Spirit has come upon you; and you shall be witnesses to Me in Jerusalem, and in all Judea and Samaria, and to the end of the earth.*

There is an obvious progression in the list of geographical locations that Jesus declares here. I believe that His purpose in listing these specific locations was to make clear that His apostolic mandate has no limitations. This mandate reaches far beyond that which is familiar to us. It's not just to the places we've always lived, but it reaches to the uttermost parts of the earth.

The point of transition for Jesus' apostles came when He was about to go back to the Father, leaving them to fulfill their mandate. They knew the message of John the Baptist. They had walked with Jesus for several years. Yet this was the moment of truth. Now they had to transition into a new apostolic season. But Jesus had prepared and equipped them. They were sent by the power of the Holy Spirit, and had everything they needed to do the job. They knew what to do. Around the world, all of creation was waiting with eager expectation. The sons of God were about to be revealed.

The funny thing is that, as we study history, we notice that the apostles were only partly successful in fulfilling their mandate. The church in Jerusalem was successfully pioneered when Peter the apostle stood up in Jerusalem on the day of Pentecost and preached the first sermon under the new covenant. Three thousand people entered the kingdom that day. Jerusalem was clearly a focus point for the early apostles. This city was mentioned by Jesus as the first place in the commission that He gave.

Yet when we read further in the book of Acts, we notice that it took years before the apostles actually went beyond the borders of Jerusalem, and began reaching to the uttermost parts of the earth. It took about fifteen years before Peter actually received the revelation that the Gospel was for the Gentiles as well as for the Jews. In Acts 10, God had to show him a vision several times before he grasped that he actually had to preach the gospel to the Gentiles. My personal belief is that the first apostles never fully transitioned into the purposes of God for their lives. They only understood the apostolic mandate in part. They preached the gospel effectively among their own people, but did not go far beyond Jerusalem. It took a second-generation apostle, Paul, to take the church to the next level of its mandate.

Paul was the first apostle to effectively minister outside of the geographical borders of Israel. This happened while all the first-generation apostles lingered in Jerusalem. But the result of their lingering was that after twenty years they still hadn't reached the Gentiles. The apostolic council had become an institution that simply maintained that which had already been established. They merely existed. There were even disputes as to whether or not Paul's ministry among the Gentiles was from God. The ironic thing was that the apostolic council was questioning the only apostle who was running with the full mandate Jesus had given by going beyond the borders of Canaan. Because of their doubts, Paul had to appear before the council and explain himself before they could give their approval. We read this story in Acts 15:1-2:

> *And certain men came down from Judea and taught the brethren, 'Unless you are circumcised according to the custom of Moses, you cannot be saved.' Therefore, when Paul and Barnabas had no small dissension and dispute with them, they determined that Paul and Barnabas and certain others of them should go up to Jerusalem, to the apostles and elders, about this question.*

This would never have been a point of discussion if they would have just listened to the words of Jesus, "Go to the uttermost parts of the earth!" How many interpretations of these words are there? There was something that kept them in Jerusalem, something that limited their ministry to the area that was familiar to them.

When we come to our point of transition, we will encounter these same dynamics. The same things that kept the apostles from fulfilling their assignment will try and keep us from fulfilling ours. But what was it that kept the apostles in Jerusalem? I believe that their limitation was the temple.

DESTROYING THE TEMPLE

Why did the temple play such an important role in Israel's history? It was the place of the manifest presence of God, and had taken an entire generation to build. For forty-six years men worked day and night, building God a dwelling place. It took their time, their money, and their energy. It was the life work of an entire generation.

The nation of Israel paid a huge price to build this temple. And then, when it was finished, their work paid off. It became the center for the majority of their religious activities. When they wanted to worship, they went to the temple. When people wanted to bring an offering, they went to the temple. The temple also played a crucial role in their national feasts. People traveled from all over to come to Jerusalem and celebrate during these feasts. Their whole spiritual experience was built around the temple. It was the place were God dwelt. For centuries, this was the order in which God established Himself. This was the way in which the people professed their faith. The temple was like an Old Testament conference center: it was the place where the priest ministered to God, and to the people. It was the place where ministry was given and received. It was the place to be. Then suddenly Jesus enters the scene and makes a shocking statement in John 2:19:

> *Jesus answered and said to them, 'Destroy this temple, and in three days I will raise it up.'*

It is imperative that we understand the impact of this statement. Jesus came to the Jews and told them to destroy the very thing—no, the only thing—that allowed them a spiritual experience. The core of their spiritual life was in the temple and its rituals. Were you to take away the temple from the Jews there would be nothing left. In their minds, if you would take away the temple, you would take away God.

Yet Jesus came and instructed them to destroy the very thing that had brought them spiritual success for so many years. He instructed them to destroy the very thing they had spent all their time, energy, and money building. But the shocking realization is that it was God Himself, the very one who had given them the orders to build, who was instructing them to tear it down!

RAISING UP THE TEMPLE

Why did Jesus tell them to destroy that which was dear to them? Did He want to be difficult? Did He just want to shock the people? Let's read John 2:19 again:

Jesus answered and said to them, 'Destroy this temple, and in three days I will raise it up.'

No, Jesus wanted the people to transition to a higher dimension. He wanted them to be part of a more complete order, of a better place. He needed to destroy in order to raise up again. This is how it always works. In order to receive the new you have to leave the old. As we read the next two verses (John 2:20-21) we'll begin to understand this new and better order:

Then the Jews said, 'It has taken forty-six years to build this temple, and will You raise it up in three days?' But He was speaking of the temple of His body.

The first thing the Jews reminded Him of was the fact that they had just spent forty-six years building the temple. But what they lacked was the understanding that the kingdom of God is one of progression and increase. They didn't understand that when God takes away the old, the new thing He does is always better. Jesus didn't want to destroy in order to rebuild the same thing. No! He wanted to rebuild a different "temple." He wanted to rebuild the temple of His body through His death and resurrection. Who is His body? The church. He is the head and we are His body. We read about this in Ephesians 5:23:

For the husband is head of the wife, as also Christ is head of the church; and He is the Savior of the body.

We also read in 1 Corinthians 6:19:

Or do you not know that your body is the temple of the Holy Spirit who is in you, whom you have from God, and you are not your own?

These two verses speak about the new season that was upon the people of Israel. They speak about the new order that Jesus wanted to establish through His death and resurrection.

Jesus didn't want to rebuild a temple of stones and mortar. He wanted to give birth to the New Testament church. No longer would God have His dwelling place in a natural building, but He would dwell in the hearts of men.

Through His death the natural temple would be destroyed. Not literally, but rather spiritually. The power of the Old Testament temple service would be lifted from a natural place, and shifted to the church, a "building" made from living stones. A transition took place in the three days that Jesus was in the grave. Then, when He arose, the laws that had been sufficient for so many years suddenly carried no weight. God had left the building!

BREAKING THE LIMITATIONS

Jesus knew that if His people would stick to the Old Testament temple order forever, that they would never fulfill His apostolic mandate. But He also understood that the physical temple was important for a season, and that it played a crucial part in God's progressive plan in history. Yet this same temple had its limitations; it was time to move on.

The limitations were clear. The temple in the Old Testament was situated in Jerusalem and bound to that location. People had to come there to receive the blessing of God. It was the only place where ministry was given and received. By rebuilding the temple in the order of the new covenant, these limitations were broken. Now there was a temple built of living stones. Wherever the church was, that's where the temple was. No longer was a spiritual experience bound to a natural location. People didn't have to travel for days to bring an offering, they could offer a sacrifice wherever they were. Jesus explains this principle to the Samaritan woman at the well. She asks Him a question in John 4:19-20:

The woman said to Him, 'Sir, I perceive that You are a prophet. Our fathers worshiped on this mountain, and you Jews say that in Jerusalem is the place where one ought to worship.'

This woman associated the place of worship with a natural location. That was what she was used to. That's how she was raised. Jesus then explained to her the transition that was about to take place. He explained to her the new order of service. No longer would she be dependent on a natural location to have a spiritual experience. We read His reaction in verse 24 of that same chapter:

God is Spirit, and those who worship Him must worship in spirit and truth.

Where do you need to worship God? On this mountain? In the temple? No, in spirit! Why would we want to go back to a building made of stone when we can worship Him in spirit today?

DAILY IN THE TEMPLE

Jesus gave the apostles a clear purpose: to preach the gospel in the uttermost parts of the earth. So why was it that they didn't fulfill His mandate? Jesus had made it clear that the limitations of the old were broken and that the "power" of the old temple was lifted. They had received power from above to go and be the church in the earth. Why did they stay in Jerusalem?

As we study the behavior pattern of the first generation, we discover something remarkable. We read the following report in Acts 5:42:

And daily in the temple, and in every house, they did not cease teaching and preaching Jesus as the Christ.

Can you believe it? They still chose the temple as their daily meeting place. Not just once in a while, but on a consistent, daily basis. What was it with that temple? Yes, theologically they embraced the fact that they could minister anywhere they wanted. That's why they also had meetings in every house, and God worked mightily by adding believers every day. Yes, they understood theologically, but they had a hard time forgetting the things of old. They had a hard time leaving the old order. The power had lifted from the physical location of the temple, and the temple itself was "destroyed," yet they still chose to gather there. Now that in itself is not bad, but I believe that there was a fear of leaving that which had always worked for them.

The temple and its habits were deeply rooted in the hearts of the people. Even the apostles were affected by it. I believe that there was the fear that, if they would leave that place, they would miss out on something. But they also had a problem. If they were really going to fulfill their apostolic mandate, they couldn't bring the temple with them to the uttermost parts of the earth. Maybe they could go to Samaria and be back for the next service, but that was about as far as they could go without leaving the temple. It was the temple that kept the apostles in

Jerusalem. It was the mindset of the old season that limited them in fulfilling their destiny. It wasn't until 70 A.D., when the temple was physically destroyed, that the apostles truly began to operate outside of the Promised Land. Even if they wanted to go to the temple, they couldn't any longer. Only when everything of the old season was destroyed were they were able to fulfill their destinies.

LEAVING OUR TEMPLE MINDSET

In order to really go with the apostolic move of God in our day, we need to be ready to radically leave behind everything that reminds us of the old season. We need to forget the things of old because God is doing a new thing. The things we did in the past, even the ways in which the church operated, are no longer valid. The apostolic church is completely different from what we are used to. Many of us have seen a certain measure of success in the old season. We did things a certain way and it worked. This will no longer be the case. The power of the old season has lifted and we have to move on. Otherwise, the blessing of yesterday will become today's limitation. If we are truly going to go to the four corners of the earth, we need to destroy the things we have built with our own hands. In this new season, the things that God once told us to build and invest in are no longer of importance because they are from a past season. We cannot go to the uttermost parts of the earth and bring with us the things from yesterday.

It is not enough to embrace theologically that God is doing something new. We need to change our old temple mindset, even if it means destroying that which is dear to us. We need to realize that if we hold on to our spiritual experiences of yesterday, they will keep us from being successful today. We are still too focused on our church buildings. We unconsciously still believe that God is more able to move in a Sunday morning church setting than on Monday morning at our work. We still communicate that the only way to be in ministry is to be behind the pulpit. In fact, a lot of the habits we have in church ministry come from previous moves of God.

For example, when we look at recent church history there was a move of God referred to as the "healing revival." Powerful men and women of God such as Oral Roberts, Paul Cain, William Branham, Jack Coe, and Kathryn Kuhlman were mightily used to heal the sick. A man by the name of T.L. Osborne came to the Netherlands and ignited a powerful revival. He had meetings in The Hague and many were healed. Thousands of people came to receive from the man of God. Extra public transportation was necessary to get everyone to the meetings. This was a powerful move of God. Because it was such a blessing, we inherited a lot of good things from this move.

As we look at the church today, we see a lot of things that come from that move. A certain order in a service, a certain style, a certain measure of faith to see God move. This is not all bad, because it worked! For example, the main strategy of these evangelists was tent campaigns. They would come into town, put up a tent, make a lot of noise, and invite people to the meetings. When you needed a miracle, you had to come to the meeting, because that's where God was moving, and He did. He would show up and confirm the word with many signs and wonders. So what do we do today when we want to reach the people in the world? We often organize a conference or a healing meeting similar to those meetings of the healing evangelists. We make a lot of noise. Why? Because that's what we are used to. That's how God moved in the previous season, so that's surely how He will move today. This is not the only example.

There are many things we do that come from an old season. It worked then, but we need to realize it's not the same today. The power has lifted off of that church system. It has been "destroyed." If your mindset is that God can only move within the borders of that "temple," than you will never leave it behind you and move into new things. Of course there is nothing wrong with tent meetings and conferences, but they should be a beginning and not an end.

The power of this current apostolic move is that we are able to do the same things those men of God did in their tent meetings wherever we are! We have been sent into the world with the same power as Christ Himself. But if our minds are not in line with this truth, we will never have the courage or compassion to pray for the sick in our workplaces, our neighborhoods or at our schools. We no longer have to wait for the man of God to come to town, but we minister whenever we are confronted with a need. Only when we destroy our temple mindset will we be able to fulfill the apostolic mandate. We have to move on! We go beyond simply gathering people in churches—we send them out in the power of the Spirit! We do this because we are not only called to maintain Jerusalem, but because we are called with a global mandate. Many times we expect the uttermost parts of the earth to come to us in Jerusalem, instead of going out.

We preach apostolic yet we still act out of our temple mind. We teach new, yet we operate out of historical habit. This needs to change. We need to come to an understanding that the destruction of the old will be the beginning of a new thing that He does in the earth.

Chapter Fourteen

POSITION YOURSELF FIRST

. . . .

GO FIRST TO JERUSALEM

One of the dimensions of the apostolic anointing is the ability to break through in the spirit realm on the highest governmental level possible. Other anointings within the fivefold spectrum carry only a certain measure of this breakthrough power, but the apostolic anointing is designed to bring down every principality of darkness on every level.

The story of King David gives us a clear picture of this type of apostolic ministry. He was the first king of Israel who actually ran with the mandate God had given him. The only man that had been king before him was Saul, and he didn't walk in the ways of the Lord throughout his entire reign. For this very reason the anointing to be king over Israel shifted from Saul to David, making him the first king in Israel who was truly obedient to will of God. In many ways, the role of a king in the Old Testament represents the role of the apostle in the New Testament. A king must rule and reign. He was created to govern and so is an apostle.

In the Old Testament, Jerusalem was the governmental seat from which the kings of old executed their reign. It was the geographic location that represented the highest place of authority. Before the kingly anointing was established in the Old Testament, the nation of Israel was being governed by Samuel the prophet, and before that by Eli the priest.

Neither the prophetic anointing nor the priestly anointing governed out of Jerusalem. Eli reigned from Shiloh, while Samuel reigned from Ramah. Both were effective, but limited in their anointing and by their geographic positioning. Both prophets had influence, yet they were never able to conquer Jerusalem, the city of kings, the city of divine government.

It wasn't until the kingly anointing was established through the life of David that Jerusalem was conquered. In fact, David's first act as king was to march up to Jerusalem and conquer the city. He knew that if he was going to be effective as king he first needed to accurately position himself. He needed to break through to a new level of government in order to bring the people of Israel to their next level of victory and freedom. It is interesting to read on and find that, after he had positioned himself in Jerusalem, everywhere he went he was successful in battle.

In the same way, a true apostle has the ability to break through to new levels of authority. He has the ability to lead and reposition the church to a higher place in the spirit. If we do not accurately position ourselves first, we will always be limited to the level of breakthrough we experienced up to that point. It is the task of the apostle to bring the church to a place of absolute victory over darkness so that, like David, we will be successful everywhere we go.

The condition for a church that wants to live in victory on a daily basis is to have breakthrough in the spirit realm. As long as demonic principalities are in place we cannot expect a move of God. Therefore we need apostles to lead us in warfare through apostolic praise and worship. Psalm 149:5-9 shows us how we can bring down the principalities of darkness through praise and worship:

Let the saints be joyful in glory; Let them sing aloud on their beds. Let the high praises of God be in their mouth. And a two-edged sword in their hand, to execute vengeance on the nations. And punishments on the peoples; to bind their kings with chains, And their nobles with fetters of iron; to execute on them the written judgment. This honor have all His saints.

We establish divine government by bringing down demonic government, and this is done through praise. Praise binds the "kings" with chains. It was through praise and worship that the ark of the covenant was ushered into Jerusalem by King David. In the same way, the ministry of the apostle will usher in the government of God through praise and worship, therefore positioning the church in a place of absolute breakthrough and victory in the spirit.

We do not only go to the enemy's camp to take back what he stole from us. That is a mindset from an old season. Actually, it is a selfish mentality, where we go to war only when we need something for ourselves. When we are sick, we go to war to take back our health. When we are broke, we go to the enemy's camp to get back our money. Once we get back what we need, we retreat until we need something again.

A true apostolic church will also go to the enemy's camp, but she won't go only with the mentality of taking back, but to overthrow the enemy, take the land, and establish the kingdom of God on the territory possessed. Her ground now becomes her dwelling place. This prevents the enemy from ever stealing from her again. Once we are in this place of authority we will not only get what we need, but will now become a source from which others can drink.

Now we will be able to start to give back the things the enemy once stole from those around us. We will be able to minister from a higher place of authority, confirming God's Word effectively with signs, wonders, and mighty deeds.

WHEN THE DAY OF PENTECOST HAD FULLY COME

It is interesting to read that the apostolic mandate Jesus gave His disciples was accompanied by another instruction. He said in Luke 24:49:

Behold, I send the Promise of My Father upon you; but tarry in the city of Jerusalem until you are endued with power from on high.

He told the apostles to go where? That's right: Jerusalem! In their cultural understanding, the city of Jerusalem was "the city of kings." It was the City of David, the place where the temple was built. It was the city from which God Himself governed His people. It was the city of authority and government. Jesus had just commissioned his disciples to go into the whole world, but first to Jerusalem. Why? To receive power! Suddenly there is a shift from a natural understanding to a spiritual understanding. Suddenly they began to understand what spiritual authority was by looking at natural examples that were given to them throughout time.

The New Testament becomes the Old Testament revealed. They began to understand that the city of Jerusalem was actually only a shadow of a spiritual place that they needed to conquer as New Testament kings. The natural Jerusalem would become the place where they would conquer the spiritual Jerusalem, resulting in a breakthrough that would endow them with power from above. They were being empowered by spiritual authority that would enable them to walk out the apostolic mandate.

But Jesus didn't want them to go out into the world without experiencing this spiritual breakthrough first. They had to come together in order to corporately break through, and from that place they were able to go out and experience the highest authority and power possible. So they waited and tarried until the promise was fulfilled. We read about it in Acts 2:1-2:

When the Day of Pentecost had fully come, they were all with one accord in one place. And suddenly there came a sound from heaven as of a rushing mighty wind, and it filled the whole house where they were sitting.

Many times we desire to see God move, yet we do not have the patience, determination, or understanding to see a spiritual breakthrough first. We want to go out while the heavens are still closed, and then we wonder why we do not experience signs and wonders. When did the apostles experience their breakthrough? Was it before the Day of Pentecost? No. Was it when the Day of Pentecost had partly come? No, it was when the Day of Pentecost had fully come! They stayed together with one accord, in one place, until they had victory in the spirit realm. They remained united in prayer until they had accurately positioned themselves. Only then did they go out and fulfill their mandate. Only then were they effective and victorious everywhere they went.

Chapter Fifteen

FULFILLING OUR MANDATE

SPIRITUAL BREAKTHROUGH NEEDS TO BE ACTED UPON

As an apostolic people we need to have an understanding of what to do with the breakthroughs we experience when we are of one accord, in one place. It is not enough just to experience the outpouring of the Holy Spirit when we come together and then go home and continue on with life as normal. Too often we go from one powerful meeting to another. I've been to so many meetings in my life, and am often frustrated as I experience a spiritual breakthrough but don't then experience the effects you would expect from it.

I can recall several meetings where there was such a heavy presence of God, such a glorious atmosphere, that I was convinced that "the revival" had finally broken out. I knew for sure that this was the beginning of the very thing we had prayed for. But then life simply continued as if nothing had happened. The breakthrough we experienced on Sunday didn't bring a clear change on Monday. Even though the heavens were opened through praise and intercession, there was no visible result afterwards. I didn't understand this for a long time, until I finally grasped that spiritual breakthroughs require initiative.

They need to be acted upon. We cannot expect a true revival to break out by being passive. Even if we're actively involved in spiritual warfare and bring down the principalities of darkness, we cannot expect the rest to happen on its own. Instead we need to work within the spiritual environment that has just been established. When the disciples came together in Jerusalem they tarried until they experienced a powerful breakthrough in the spirit. Once they had experienced this, they didn't just sit and wait and let God do the rest. We see a different response, in Acts: 2:14:

> *But Peter, standing up with the eleven, raised his voice and said to them.*

Peter was anything but passive after he experienced a spiritual breakthrough. He stood up and raised his voice. He understood that he had to work with what was established in the heavenly realm. He understood that the heavens were now open, and he used this opportunity to work out his mandate of preaching the gospel. He went from the upper room to outside, and began to preach the gospel of Jesus Christ to those who had not been a part of his breakthrough meeting.

This is an important lesson. We cannot live from meeting to meeting, or from breakthrough to breakthrough, without building in between. We need to work with what we have already established in the spirit realm. If principalities are brought down on Sunday, we should use that breakthrough to stand up and do something. If we pray for miracles on Sunday and see that we have torn down a stronghold of the enemy, then we had better go out on Monday and pray for the sick. In this way we seal our breakthrough and benefit from it in the long term.

Too often we fight the same battles over and over again. We intercede at one meeting, go home and do nothing. Then, by the time we go to the next meeting, the enemy has repositioned himself, and we fight that same battle again. We shouldn't allow this to happen any longer. Every victory in the realm of the spirit requires initiative from the saints of God if we want to reap the long-term fruit of it.

THE WORK OF THE MINISTRY

The frontlines of the true apostolic church are not meetings on a Sunday morning. In fact, the biggest action takes place throughout the week, making Sundays a celebration of the things that the Lord has done in our lives throughout the week. A true apostolic saint knows how to walk in his apostolic authority twenty-four hours a day, seven days a week. Therefore, the result of the true apostolic move will be that every saint of God—not just the church leadership—will become effective for the kingdom.

Several years ago, a friend of mine had a vision in which he saw a soccer stadium. It had five rings where people could sit and watch the game. God spoke to him that each of the five rings represented one of the fivefold ministry gifts. These rings were focused on the inside of the stadium , where the game was being played. But then something strange happened. Suddenly the stadium was twisting and turning, causing the whole building to be turned inside out. No longer were the five rings focused on the game inside of the stadium, but they were turned to the outside. Suddenly those seated in the five rings realized that there was another game needing to be played. The action was no longer inside the stadium, but outside.

This vision impressed me so much that even today I clearly remember every detail. We are not involved in playing a game isolated from the world around us. The game takes place in the world around us. We need to shift our focus 180 degrees. Let's go back to Ephesians 4:11-12, which talks about the fivefold ministry:

And He Himself gave some to be apostles, some prophets, some evangelists, and some pastors and teachers, for the equipping of the saints, for the work of ministry.

Why do we have fivefold ministers? They are given so that the saints might be equipped for the work of ministry. So then who are the real ministers? That's right, the saints!

For too long we have had an inward focus, trying to get the world to come to our "stadium" so that the fivefold leadership could minister to them. We've been busy trying to figure out structures and strategies to make church accessible for unbelievers, thinking that if we could only get them in, then we could expose them to true ministry. I believe that this mentality is an invention of the devil himself. Sometimes we think that by changing our church structure to work with cell groups that church is not so intimidating on Sundays. Then maybe they will come, or so we think.

However, whatever programs we come up with, they will not work within the context of apostolic reformation. We can come up with seeker-sensitive programs. We can even come up with different cell group strategies. The bottom line is that our focus needs to shift from "inviting the world to come" to "sending the church to go." We need to realize that the action is outside the stadium, not inside. The saints of God need to be equipped. They need to come forth and be powerful in their ministry to the people around them. We should all be ministers in the kingdom of God.

SOWING SONS OF THE KINGDOM

To confront the wrong mindset we've had concerning church growth from another angle, let's look at Matthew 13:24-30:

> *Another parable He put forth to them, saying: 'The Kingdom of heaven is like a man who sowed tares among the wheat and went his way. But when the grain had sprouted and produced a crop, then the tares also appeared. So the servants of the owner came and said to him, Sir, did you not sow good seed in your field? How then does it have tares? He said to them, An enemy has done this. The servants said to him, Do you want us then to go and gather them up? But he said, No, lest while you gather up the tares you also uproot the wheat with them. Let both grow together until the harvest, and at the time of the harvest I will say to the reapers, First gather together the tares and bind them in bundles to burn them,*

but gather the wheat into my barn.'

Later on Jesus explains the parable to his disciples in verses 37-38:

> *He answered and said to them: 'He who sows the good seed is the Son of Man. The field is the world, the good seeds are the sons of the Kingdom, but the tares are the sons of the wicked one.'*

We see here that there are sons of the kingdom, represented by the good seed. There are also the sons of the wicked one, represented by the tares. Both are being sown into the field by their master, with the field representing the earth. Both the Son of Man, as well as the evil one, will sow sons into the world to bear fruit; the good and the bad seed are mixed up in the field. Notice the question that was asked instantly when the servants of the Son of Man noticed that evil and good were sown together in the same field.

They asked, "Do you want us then to go and gather them up?" This is a question that reveals a profound truth about our wrong mindset. So often we try to separate the sons of the kingdom from the sons of the wicked one because we are afraid they will negatively influence us.

Too often the result is that the church becomes an isolated organization, separated from normal life. We do not realize that we, the church, are given the power and mandate to influence them. The instruction of the Son of Man is the opposite of what his servants expected: "Let both grow until the harvest." If we want to see a harvest, we must leave the sons of the kingdom among the sons of the wicked one until the harvest time. Yes, there will still be a harvest when both grow up together. But instead, what we have done is isolated the sons of the kingdom in their little stadium, as opposed to yielding ourselves to our Master and allowing Him to effectively plant us in the field, allowing us to grow until the harvest time.

DESCENDING THE MOUNTAIN

We cannot simply stand on the walls of our church buildings and call the people to come. They will not. We need to actually be among those that need Christ. We need to be among the harvest. We need to leave our comfort zones, go to their level first, and then take them by the hand and lead them. But first we have to go out.

When Moses was having a meeting with God, He gave him a major revelation (the Ten Commandments) that would direct the people of Israel for centuries. Yet Moses didn't shout out this wonderful revelation from the top of the mountain. Instead, he chose to descend the mountain and meet the people at their level, and from that place communicate the things God had revealed to him. In the same way we too must descend from our spiritual mountain, coming to the level of the people around us, and effectively minister from that place.

ORDINARY PEOPLE DOING EXTRAORDINARY THINGS

Too often, when someone becomes a Christian, while he is all exited and going for it, we tell him that the world has a bad influence on him, and that he has to be freed from a lot of stuff. We tell him that he needs to prioritize his life. So we explain that on Monday there is a prayer meeting. He won't only get to pray, but will also receive teaching on how to pray for his unsaved friends. On Wednesday we have cell group.

We explain that because the cell group is small, it is easy to invite a friend or neighbor to it. That way they will hear the gospel in a relaxed atmosphere. On Thursday we will go onto the streets to evangelize. We will talk to people about Jesus Christ. On Friday we have Bible study night, and on Sunday we have our weekly service. We explain that it would be good if he could come to all of the meetings, so that a good foundation can be laid.

So this new Christian is listening to his new week's schedule and starts to think, how he can work this out? Normally on Monday he goes to soccer practice, and on Wednesday he always plays cards with the neighbors. Thursday nights he usually goes shopping with a friend, and on Friday he stays at work late to have some fun with his colleagues before the weekend starts. What should he do?

After thinking about and wrestling with this question, he finally decides to go with the church schedule. He needs to know how to pray for his friends correctly, so he has to go to the prayer meeting. Also, the

Wednesday night meeting would be good, and maybe after a few weeks he'll invite his card-playing friends. And on and on he goes. Now, don't get me wrong. A newborn Christian needs to become clean and strong. And yes, that takes time. But by forcing a totally new weekly schedule in his life, we basically extract him from normal society. It won't be long before the connections he had within society will be lost forever. And all of this, just to teach him how to be an effective Christian that will lead people into the kingdom. But in reality, it's we who have to adjust our mindset. We need to keep the sons of the kingdom in the field. Why do we spend all our time figuring out the right strategy and structure for drawing the world into the kingdom of God, when the mandate is to go out to them?

Maybe, instead of restructuring the church to make her more accessible for non-believers, we should focus on equipping the believers we already have. As we've already read in Ephesians 4, the fivefold ministry is called to equip the saints. Church meetings are for the saints, not for unbelievers. Whenever fivefold ministers have meetings, the focus should be on equipping those that are already saved. The anointing of the fivefold ministry is designed to equip. It is created to enable the saints to do the work of the ministry. Outreach and evangelism most definitely have a place, but should occur outside and not inside the church.

With this understanding, why then would we extract believers from society? Isn't it better to leave them where God's

placed them? Let them have their card game nights and soccer practices. Rather, equip them! Let them be ordinary people with ordinary relationships. We need to realize that every
person who is just born again has an entire natural network of
relationships.

If we would just spend the time we have equipping them,
instead of extracting them, we would probably experience a
tremendously effective and explosive means of evangelism.
Church leaders wouldn't have to do the work of the ministry
all by themselves anymore. All they would do is equip. Leaders
would no longer have to strategize on how to bring unbelievers
into the church. We wouldn't have to think about how to reach
certain people groups, or how to interact on different levels of
society. After all, the people in our churches would represent
all those we would be trying to reach.

The fivefold ministry will have already equipped ordinary
people with ordinary relationships to be ministers of the gospel. Suddenly the saints will be the ones who are well able to
do the work of the ministry. Suddenly these ordinary people
with ordinary lives will begin doing extraordinary things.
They'll start to minister to the people they practice with on
soccer nights. They won't have to invite them to a meeting
first, but will minister right where they are. They won't have
to worry whether or not their teammates will show up for the
next church meeting because everyone always practices on
Monday nights, and so they'll all be there.

These equipped saints will minister in their environment
because they'll already be planted in their field. Their natural network of relationships has just become their sphere of
influence and authority. It has become their mission field.
And because they will also be equipped, they'll be able to lead
their friends and teammates to Christ themselves. And then,
after all of that, they'll be able to ask them to go with them to
church, because by this time they are already saved! With this
organic church structure, we won't need to have all kinds of
complicated outreaches, because the church will already be

reaching out. The saints will be equipped to do the work of the ministry. This is the church that will be effective on the front-lines of the army of God, experiencing victory after victory.

CROSSING THE JORDAN, RELEASING THE SAINTS

Equipping the saints should be the ultimate purpose of church leadership. Leaders have been given to the church in order to bring ordinary people to their destiny. Spiritual leaders have been positioned to release the saints into their inheritance, and to lead them to success on every level. Remember that God doesn't do anything unless He first reveals it to His servants, the prophets. This is why it's so important for us to follow. Not just for the sake of following, but because the road we are walking will often lead us into the unknown.

As we have discussed, a lot of people have difficulty submitting to the leadership of men of God because doing so requires a humble attitude. In the same way, true leadership is not about who is the boss and who is not. It is about operating in a God-given function that serves a specific purpose. This purpose is to equip and release the saints. Let's read the account of Joshua again and be amazed at how his instruction for everyone to follow the priests to the river Jordan ultimately served the purpose of releasing everyone into their destiny. Joshua 3:14-17 says:

So it was, when the people set out from their camp to cross over the Jordan, with the priests bearing the ark of the covenant before the people, and as those who bore the ark came to the Jordan, and the feet of the priests who bore the ark dipped in the edge of the water that the waters which cam down from upstream stood still and rose in a heap very far away at Adam, the city that is beside Zaretan. So the waters that went down into the sea of the Arabah, the Salt Sea, failed, and were cut off; and the people crossed over opposite Jericho. Then the priests who bore the ark of the covenant of the Lord stood firm on dry ground in the midst of the Jordan; an all Israel crossed over on dry ground, until all the people had crossed completely over the Jordan.

This is a great example of how leadership serves the purpose of equipping and releasing the saints. Remember, from the time the Israelites were in Egypt up until this point, it was the leader who formed the frontline of progression. Their leader had led them through the wilderness, across the Red Sea and beyond the enemy's territory. And it was their leader who had finally brought them to the Jordan.

However, the river separated them from their destiny and the Promised Land. This was the last obstacle that needed to be taken. Joshua gave the instruction to follow the priests, and again they chose to follow. Then a profound shift took place. The leading priests who bore the ark of the covenant of the Lord suddenly stood firm on dry ground in the middle of the river. The interesting thing is that the people following didn't follow their stand. Instead, all of Israel crossed over on dry ground, until all the people had crossed completely over the Jordan.

This is a powerful thing. The Jordan was before them, and the priests were taking their place at the front of a long line of Israelites. These priests, these leaders, had been leading the people for years through all the difficult stages of their costly journey. Now, when they had finally come to the land of promise, what did these great men of God do? They removed the last obstacle that would have kept the people from their promise, releasing them into destiny. They stood still and let the people cross over on dry ground. In other words, they began at the front but were the last ones to end up on the other side. They had completed a big part of their purpose. They had led the people of Israel to the Promised Land, and then released them at the border, allowing them to be released into their destiny.It was the ordinary Israelites that set foot in the Promised Land first.

This is very important to note, because the apostolic move will ultimately release ordinary believers into their land of promise in the same way, shifting leadership more to the background and allowing the saints to do the work of the ministry. Of course leadership will always remain important and vital, but their role will shift from only leading, to leading and releasing. This empowering of the saints will be the characteristic of the true apostolic move, as every saint of God will arise and be revealed as a son of God.

CONCLUSION

We are living in a time of destiny. An apostolic awareness is saturating the church of Jesus Christ. This awareness is changing mindsets, structures, and doctrine. Christians all over the world are beginning to realize that we live in a time in which the sons of God are being revealed in the earth. This is the time where every believer will be powerful and effective in the kingdom of God. We are all called with an apostolic call, commissioned to change the nations. We know that we have the power to change history.

As the saints of God arise in this time, nations will be impacted spiritually, socially, and economically. A true transformation will take place in the different regions of the earth.

These are exiting times: let the saints of God arise!

For more information on the apostolic move and on Martijn van Tilborgh go to *www.martijnvantilborgh.com.* Other books from Martijn van Tilborgh are:

Chronicles of Reformation
The War on the Male Child

Available Online!